The New Data Imperative

Managing Real-time Risk in Capital Markets

Dr. Raj Nathan

Irfan Khan

Sinan Baskan

EASTON STUDIO PRESS

2009

ISBN 10-1-935212-03-6
ISBN 13-978-1-935212-03-4

978-1-935212-04-1 e-book editions

Published by
Easton Studio Press
P.O. Box 3131
Westport, CT 06880
Printed in the United States of America
June 2009

Book design and composition by Mark McGarry,
Texas Type & Book Works

10 9 8 7 6 5 4 3 2 1

Mixed Sources

Product group from well-managed forests, controlled sources and recycled wood or fibre

www.fsc.org   Cert no. SGS-COC-005368
© 1996 Forest Stewardship Council

FSC

Acknowledgments

The seeds of The New Data Imperative: Managing Real-time Risk in Capital Markets were sown a year ago when Sybase employees began discussing how the company might offer ideas to help sweep away the chaos in the financial sector. Listing three authors of this book is one thing, but several other people made notable contributions in developing and refining the expression of our thoughts. Mark Wilson, Robyn Albarran and Chris Forsyth each contributed to the ideas in the book. We owe particular thanks also to David Wilk, the publisher, and to Hilary Hinzmann, the editor, for their dedication and thoughtfulness.

Contents

Foreword

Today's financial turmoil has guaranteed one thing for sure: Information technology will be critical to the success of how capital markets companies in a highly interconnected world manage risk in the future to generate profit.

IT not only empowers capital markets companies to operate as they do, it is also a critical source of competitive advantage. IT systems are so much at the core of what capital markets companies do, that it can be argued that better IT could have mitigated the risks they took while they collected, invested and distributed money in the lead-up to the credit crisis.

When Lloyd Blankfein told the U.S. Senate Banking Committee early in 2009 that "we cannot let our ability to innovate exceed our capacity to manage," the chief executive of Goldman Sachs was alluding to the fact that a company's ability to introduce innovations should not get ahead of its managing the consequences. In fact, Goldman managed the innovation process better than most to reduce risk relatively early in markets and instruments that were deteriorating. Yet much the same information available to Goldman was available to everyone else. Clearly, sophisticated use of that information was more an exception than the rule in most companies in spite of large databases and even larger data warehouses.

The lesson is obvious.

History may judge the bankruptcy of Lehman Brothers as the shock that changed the capital markets forever. Lehman's failure was all the more profound because it was considered to have the risk management systems and balance sheet management practices to withstand even a magnitude-10 earthquake. Investigations by numerous experts into what went wrong in the markets in the past 18 months or so have concluded that organizational "silos" that prevented institutions from having an enterprise view of risk were at least partly to blame.

Previous recessions occurred when the IT infrastructure of the capital markets was relatively primitive compared to what exists today, and information flows were far less rapid and large. Today, information comes in torrents virtually in "real time" and relatively cheaply. Against this backdrop, recent advances in IT infrastructures such as enterprisewide systems are capable of overcoming the barriers imposed by silos to the flow of information across-the-board.

And then there is regulation. To drive the capital markets to a collective remedy for what went wrong, Blankfein and others have called for effective central regulation. In response, Commissioner Elisse B. Walter of the U.S. Securities and Exchange Commission said in a speech in New York in Feb. 2009 that she believed IT had a vital role in modernizing the disclosure system under federal securities law and in promoting transparency, liquidity and efficiency in the capital markets.

The steps being taken by various governments around the world to reverse the current economic downturn coincide with advances in IT that will cause the public—and regulators—to expect more frequent, even continuous, business reporting and more effective risk management. While there will be many surprises to come, there is no doubt that as one of the most dynamic and innovative industries in existence IT will have a significant role to play in rebuilding the trust and confidence that are so necessary for the effective operation of the capital markets.

IT is not only critical to the future operations of the capital markets, but is also a vital contributor to growth in the economy as a whole. Historically, innovations in IT that have improved crisis resolution mechanisms have been a key driver of global productivity growth. In fact, IT change and related organizational and production improvements more than doubled their contributions to the gross domestic product in the United States between 1995–2004, compared with 1980–1995.

By taking advantage of what IT has to offer in the way of managing current and anticipated future business models in the capital markets and maintaining them as a place to put money to work and depend on the outcome, we could be well on the way to generating long-term gain once again.

RICH KARLGAARD
Publisher of Forbes magazine

Introduction

As we get deeper into 2009, the consequences of the financial crisis and structural changes in capital markets will impact the economy and capital markets companies. With that awareness we at Sybase pondered how the information technology industry—and Sybase as a provider of risk management technology—can help promote stability, growth and prudent governance within the capital markets. This book is the result.

The extreme distress caused by the worldwide financial crunch has focused attention on who did or did not see it coming and generated the perception that something unprecedented has happened. Among those who did see it coming is Bob Rodriquez, CEO at the mutual fund First Pacific Advisors, who told the Wall Street Journal in January 2009 that what we're facing has "no historical precedent."

Compare our current situation with the historical record of past crises, however, and it does reveal a common pattern. Time and again risky plays outstrip the checks and balances of the financial system, and irrational exuberance outstrips common sense and know-how. In fact, we may be repeating a well-established pattern, albeit more severely, as the following pages will explore to draw lessons for the difficult days ahead.

The evolution of the capital markets over recent years has seen trading and portfolio decisions increasingly shaped by a model-driven, data-intensive approach deploying innovative products and new technology. Overall, financial computer models have been helpful in managing securitization and financial risks. But they don't work indefinitely with bad data, or as the saying goes, "Garbage in, garbage out."

In the subprime meltdown excessively optimistic assumptions, oversimplification of interrelationships and incomplete data blinded all too many organizations to the risks they were running. They lied to their computers, is how the New York Times put it in Sept. 2008. The result is that their computers weren't there to warn them when necessary.

Models work best when observed behavior emulates well-understood statistical patterns. But financial markets don't always conform to such patterns over extended periods. Unanticipated events and all interconnected and interrelated behavior cannot be forecast in advance, especially in a globalized world. Model-driven analytical support systems are like a compass or a GPS device. They're invaluable for finding directions—and anyone trying to function without them is at a woeful competitive disadvantage—but someone still needs to be looking at them from the correct perspective. Where capital markets portfolio and risk management are involved, analytical support systems need to be designed for decision makers who have the perspective and authority to make the tough calls.

The question now is, will the financial crisis change the structure of markets in a radical and lasting way? "History demonstrates conclusively that a modern economy cannot grow if its financial system is not operating effectively." So said Ben Bernanke, the U.S. Federal Reserve chairman, in London in Jan. 2009.

Prior changes in the nature of markets, regulations and technology created an environment where proper understanding of market dynamics and the ability to see the warning signs were obscured in the financial data that is at the very core of profitability.

More data than ever is generated in financial markets, and capital markets firms increasingly depend upon receiving reliable information quickly. Once gathered, this information must just as quickly be made available for business analysis, decision making, internal governance and regulatory compliance.

No one has yet found a way to make money without taking risks. But organizations must be confident about their exposure to risk and the true valuations of their portfolios. The objective, therefore, must be to manage risk. "We cannot respond to every accident by trying to guarantee ever more tiny margins of safety. We cannot eliminate risk. We have to live with it," then British Prime Minister Tony Blair said in a speech to the Institute of Public Policy Research four years ago in London.

If we define risk as quantifiable uncertainty, then it is manageable with sufficient data on causality and correlations. Financial institutions accordingly must be able to integrate long-term trend data and relevant current information to create a single view of the truth. This is only possible when markets function efficiently. Efficient markets are critical to understanding investment risks and seeking returns in proportion to those risks. Managing risk also requires a global perspective not only to bring companies through the present crisis, but also to lay the foundations to succeed in the future. Managing risk is not merely about designing quantitative models with the inevitable assumptions and the accompanying theoretical constructs, nor is it solely about processes, procedures and reporting cycles. The liquidity crisis and subsequent events showed that at least some risk management practices were fundamentally flawed by what they ignored. Factors such as earning power, growth rates, different pricing dynamics of real and traded assets, and consumer behavior may not be easy to quantify, but every economy has limits that must always frame decisions about capital allocation. A more contextual, holistic approach to modeling might have helped.

Our view is that properly presented data can help expose the causes behind market behavior more immediately and effectively. As organizations seek better governance and improved risk management, their chief risk and compliance officers will need more granular data on asset prices and market interactions. They will also face demands for an increased focus on balance sheet management and accurate and timely collateral valuations. If we look at past crises, what's likely to emerge is a restructured capital markets system with greater transparency, tighter controls on portfolio trading practices and more rigorous regulatory oversight. Hopefully, these measures will help drive a recovery, as they have after past crises, and be only a small price to pay for individual players.

Given the essential resilience of the global economy, there will be a recovery sooner or later.

A shift is under way in favor of managing capital and financial risks under a balance sheet management model rather than at the level of transaction-driven business units. This will require a more data-centric approach and more effective management of information flow. IT is charged to engineer this shift and Sybase is looking to expedite it. This is needed for measured risk-taking, the foundation for growth in capital markets. Our objective is to make a positive difference along the way, enabling insight to support informed decisions and confident actions. We hope that this book will contribute significantly to meeting those ends.

JOHN CHEN
Chairman, CEO and President, Sybase, Inc.

The New Data Imperative

Chapter 1

The Background: Information and Risk

PAUL VOLCKER, director of President Barack Obama's Economic Advisory Council, is one of a number of authoritative figures to observe that over the past quarter of a century the function of global financial intermediation and capital allocation has steadily moved from a commercial-bank-centered, highly regulated system to a vastly more complex engineered system that has operated beyond effective oversight and governance. Most capital inflows are realized through trading derivative instruments that the legacy governance structures are not capable of tracking.

This transformation blindsided regulatory governance to a degree and obscured warning signs of pending trouble. Instead, regulatory bodies and agencies largely depended on financial firms themselves to assess the risks they were running in a fiercely competitive market, where failure to play the game as others were doing might incur a penalty in stock price rather than a premium for careful risk management.

In a letter to all financial institutions active in the credit derivatives market in February 2005, for example, an official of Britain's Financial Services Authority wrote: "We ask you to consider your firm's operational processes and risk management frameworks—and the resourcing of these in relation to credit derivatives—to assess their robustness in this rapidly evolving market."

Since late 2007, we've seen a steady stream of dire news in capital markets and the impact of the original subprime crisis is now, due to the restriction of credit, manifest in other sectors of the U.S. economy as well as globally.

As of early Aug. 2008 five of the largest investment banks had reported write-offs totaling $132.8 billion and raised funds from external sources amounting to $100 billion (see Table 1).

Citigroup had CDO (collateralized debt obligations) exposure that was repriced at 53 percent on the dollar. Morgan Stanley was facing $1.5 billion of CDO exposure with a paid-in capital of $34 billion and $69 billion of assets on the balance sheet that had yet to be repriced. Prior to filing for bankruptcy protection, Lehman Brothers had $72 billion in mortgages with $21 billion of these assets deemed impossible to revalue against a capital of $26 billion.

Media and other discussion of the path that led to the current state of affairs naturally focuses on the domino effect of subprime mortgage–lending practices and the securitization of loan portfolios. Indeed, Meredith Whitney, the equity analyst at

Oppenheimer & Co. renowned for early warnings about leading financial institutions' exposure to the subprime market, expects a long-lasting impact on the general economy due to the questionable practices of the ratings agencies that issued inflated ratings on subprime-backed securities (Fortune, Aug.18, 2008, p. 68). About $85 billion in mortgage securities were downgraded in Q3 of 2007. This was followed by $237 billion in Q4, $739 billion in Q1 2008 and $841 billion in Q2. The capital lost and tied up in reserves to shore up balance sheets is a primary cause of the credit crunch. By the end of 2008 the reported losses and provisions from leading institutions reached extraordinary levels (see Figure 1).

After the full extent of the credit crisis could no longer be ignored, many asked why it was not widely acknowledged and resolved early on. In fact, a number of well-placed observers tried to sound the alarm. In addition to Ms. Whitney, they include professor Nouriel Roubini of NYU, Sean Egan of Egan-Jones Ratings and money managers David Einhorn and

Table 1: All Together

Institution	Write-downs (in billions, USD)	Capital Raised (in billions, USD)	Change in Bond Ratings
Citigroup	54.6	49.1	AA to AA-
Merrill Lynch	51.8	30.8	AA- to A
Morgan Stanley	14.4	5.6	AA- to A+
Lehman Brothers	8.2	13.9	A+ to A
Goldman Sachs	3.8	0.6	AA- unchanged

Source: Crain's New York Business, Aug. 4, 2008

Figure 1: Write-downs as of 2008

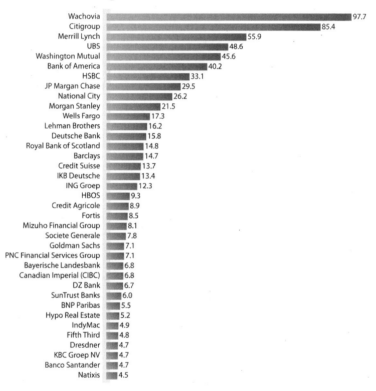

Write-downs reported as of end of 2008, since the beginning of 2007. Credit losses include increases in bad loan provisions, net of financial hedges.

Source: Bloomberg. Analysis by TowerGroup

Robert Rodriquez. Another in this group is money manager Peter Schiff, author of "Crash Proof: How to Profit from the Coming Economic Collapse." A frequent commentator on the financial news networks who has earned the nickname "Dr. Doom," Schiff said in an Aug. 2006 interview: "The United States economy is like the Titanic and I am here with the lifeboat trying to get people to leave the ship ... I see a real financial crisis coming for the United States." On May 16, 2006, Schiff accurately forecast on a news network that the U.S. housing market was a bubble that would soon burst.

Ahead of them all, perhaps, was the late Edmund M. Gramlich, a Federal Reserve governor who warned about eight years ago that a fast-growing new breed of lenders was luring many people into risky mortgages they could not afford, according to New York Times reporter Edmund Andrews ("Fed Shrugged as Subprime Crisis Spread," Dec. 18, 2007). But when Gramlich privately urged Fed examiners to investigate mortgage lenders affiliated with national banks, he was rebuffed by then Fed chairman Alan Greenspan. Likewise, when senior Treasury official Sheila C. Bair, now head of the FDIC, tried in 2001 to persuade subprime lenders to adopt a code of "best practices" and to let outside monitors verify their compliance, none of the lenders would agree to the monitors and many rejected the code itself. Even those who did adopt those practices soon let them slip, Ms. Bair recalled in an interview with Massachusetts, the magazine of the Massachusetts Bankers Association. In 2004 John C. Gamboa and Robert L. Gnaizda, leaders of a housing advocacy group in California, met the same disinclination to confront looming troubles when they implored Greenspan to use his bully pulpit to press for a voluntary code of conduct to limit unscrupulous subprime lending.

Those who saw trouble ahead and those who failed to do so had access to the same data. But hindsight shows that they were not equally able to draw good information from that data. In light of this, it is worth asking how much of the difference is owing to human nature—we see what we are willing to see—and how much is owing to inadequate financial information systems. We can begin to weigh the balance of these factors by asking whether the current credit crisis is, as the fevered nature of much press commentary might suggest, truly a new phenomenon.

In two recent research papers, economics professors Carmen Reinhart (University of Maryland) and Ken Rogoff (Harvard University) argue that this crisis in fact follows a familiar pattern ("Is the 2007 U.S. Sub-Prime Financial Crisis So Different? An International Historical Comparison," published in Feb. 2008 and "This Time Is Different: A Panoramic View of Eight Centuries of Financial Crisis," NBER working paper 13882, March 2008). Ahead of each financial crisis in modern history real prices rose sharply followed by securities traded in capital markets, they observe. Both current account deficits and public debt rose simultaneously over an extended period of time; concurrently, capital inflows in specific sectors of the economy accelerated while overall economic growth slowed steadily. Almost without exception these crises followed a period of deregulation or reformist activism in financial markets.

Another characteristic that the current crisis shares with past events is the relatively rapid spread of its impact across national boundaries. Every major financial crisis since maritime navigation first dominated global trade has reached international scale before being brought under control.

Also, most asset price bubbles follow long periods of low inflation and price stability, in which investors seek higher returns on their accumulated assets by raising their risk tolerance, regardless of the capability to price investment risk. And each period of global economic expansion was driven by key innovations in the financial markets. The evolution of the global financial system thus shows a lagging push-pull dynamic between new forms of investment and understanding of their inherent risks.

Professors Reinhart and Rogoff found that the average drop in real per capita output growth in all the postwar recessions was over 2 percent and typically took two years to return to normal growth in spite of the complicated interactions between the triggering impetus and policy response, hardly a staggering decline.

Among the 18 previous post–World War II banking crises in industrial countries, Reinhart and Rogoff highlight "Five Big Crises," catastrophic periods where the drop in annual output growth from peak to trough was over 5 percent and growth remained well below the precrisis trend even after three years. "These more catastrophic cases, of course, mark the boundary that policy makers want to avoid," the authors note. The Big Five Crises occurred in Spain (starting year 1977), Norway

(1987), Finland (1991), Sweden (1991) and Japan (1992). The remainder studied were in Australia (1989), Canada (1983), Denmark (1987), France (1994), Germany (1977), Greece (1991), Iceland (1985), Italy (1990), New Zealand (1987), United Kingdom (1974, 1991, 1995) and the United States (1984, the savings and loan crisis).

Reinhart and Rogoff conclude that although each crisis is distinct, the Big Five share striking similarities in the run-up of asset prices, debt accumulation, growth patterns and current account deficits. The majority are preceded by financial liberalization. "The first major financial crisis of the 21st century involves esoteric instruments, unaware regulators, and skittish investors," they write. And in so doing, "It ... follows a well-trodden path laid down by centuries of financial folly."

As professors Reinhart and Rogoff point out, although technology, fashions and even the height of humans has changed over the years, the ability of government and investors to delude themselves hasn't. This points to the need for improving financial information systems as a basis for decision making by financial institutions, investors and regulatory bodies. The need becomes more urgent as the links and interdependencies among market players become more complex and more immediate.

Commenting on the subprime crisis in Fortune on April 28, 2008, Warren Buffet, the chairman of Berkshire Hathaway, said, "Finance has gotten so complicated, with so much interdependency ... What you have done is interconnected the solvency of institutions to a degree that probably nobody anticipated." He also suggested that even if one assumes that risks are accurately priced relative to the given economic and fiscal environment, the layers of securitization have created a different kind of dependency.

Bruce Wasserstein, chairman and CEO of Lazard, sounded a similar note in April 2008. "We know that the pace of change is accelerating, and that requires even more adroit adaptation on the part of the market and regulators," he said. "Financial technology has outpaced our common sense in absorbing it. In the last 10 years the banks have innovated an array of financial devices, which were brilliant in their conceptualization, and in the early days were disciplined by a due diligence process for the underlying securities. But in their evolved forms, the knowledge of what these innovations were being wrapped around got lost. So it's not shocking that there are cracks in the system. What is surprising is the sheer size and high proportion of risky bets that were made."[1]

There is no doubt that the trading of asset-backed derivative instruments has become highly complex and intractable. It may even be argued that market complexity has advanced beyond any one firm's current capacity to price risk properly. The interplay of trading risk across financial institutions creates a challenging environment for capital markets firms and policy makers alike. Although the phenomenon may be qualitatively appreciated, a far more accurate quantitative understanding is essential for both profitable trading operations and appropriate regulatory response.

The solvency of the entire financial system, as well as individual firms, requires integration of information on linked asset classes, price and volatility correlations between traded instruments and underlying assets and, last but not least, counterparty data. Accurate assessment of exposure to the balance sheet and risk pricing makes it imperative that the information flow from source to decision maker be robust and reliable.

Although information technology architectures have made it possible for financial firms to handle the large increases in data on trades that have been recorded and to evaluate shifting investment positions much faster than previously, the industry needs to take greater strides in adopting innovative architectures, technologies and processes to manage risk effectively. According to Robert Shiller, the economist whose book "Irrational Exuberance" analyzed the technology stock bubble, and who together with his colleague Karl Case originated the S&P/Case Shiller Home Price Index, what's needed to solve the subprime meltdown is better information, including improved consumer education, with new risk management technologies coupled with a new futures market in housing that improves price transparency.[2] All observers agree that poorly informed consumer behavior and lack of transparency in lending practices have played a major role in distorting asset and credit pricing.

The International Organization of Securities Commissions (IOSCO), a global market watchdog, has also highlighted the "inadequate human and technological resources" that helped spark the subprime crisis. It is evident that advances in technology and human skill need to be in appropriate synchronization. When know-how and judgment lag behind as they do now, then it is more imperative that the technology environment compensate for this gap. For example, the risk measurement and pricing methodology will need to make up for inadequate information, limited understanding of the markets and procedural deficiencies through improved integration of data and more complete, deep history on process and volatilities.

Consider the implications of the New York Times headline on Sept. 18, 2008, "How Wall Street Lied to Its Computers" above an article written by Saul Hansell. After interviewing Wall Street information technology veterans, of which he is one, he explained that most Wall Street computer models radically underestimated the risk of complex mortgage securities. "That is partly because the level of financial distress is 'the equivalent of the 100-year flood,' in the words of Leslie Rahl, the president of Capital Market Risk Advisors, a consulting firm. But she and others say there is more to it: The people who ran the financial firms chose to program their risk-management systems with overly optimistic assumptions and to use oversimplified data. This kept them from sounding the alarm early enough."

To the same point, Alan Greenspan testified in Congress (Oct. 23, 2008) on the effects of an information gap in the industry that was not previously apparent to him and many others. "The best insights of mathematicians and finance experts, supported by major advances in computer and communications technology" had a fatal flaw, he said. "The whole intellectual edifice collapsed in the summer of last year because the data inputted into the risk management models generally covered only the past two decades, a period of euphoria."

Perfect market information is of course impossible in our imperfect world. Portfolio and financial risk management decision cycles are therefore critical to managing the balance sheet and ultimately the profitability of firms in the capital markets. The analyses and decisions made within a decision cycle require a balance in both content and temporal coherence. Five variable factors, each the dimension of a frame of reference, determine the quality of portfolio and risk management decisions. These dimensions represent business goals, organizational capabilities, internal processes and practices and the regulatory environment as follows:

- **Portfolio structure and financial performance targets:** This dimension includes processes and decisions that determine portfolio allocations, asset class and instrument trading at the desks, including proprietary trading, and assets that are carried on the balance sheet. It also includes decisions on securitization and issuance. The choice of instruments, which may be complex structured products, and of trading and hedging strategies is based on target portfolio returns and overall profitability goals
- **Risk targets and exposure tolerance:** This dimension covers risk management practices and metrics by asset class, portfolio and aggregated risk to traded capital. Balance sheet management and product control processes and decisions fall into this category
- **Regulatory and compliance processes and requirements:** This category includes internal controls and compliance

processes as well as regulatory and financial reporting. Workflows and practices that generate demand for both expertise and infrastructure are scaled along this dimension

- **Business organization and workflow architecture:** This dimension represents the human resources, organizational structure and procedures needed to fulfill the requirements generated by the first three dimensions
- **Technology infrastructure:** This dimension represents the technological capabilities, expertise, and human and physical resources needed to fulfill the technical requirements generated by the first four dimensions

These five dimensions contribute to successful management of traded capital and balance sheet exposure while achieving profitability and regulatory targets. They can be depicted as a set of five vectors that begin in the center of a pentagon, with the corners of the pentagon depicting the targets (see Figure 2a). Though the vectors are not entirely independent of one another, they represent functional areas that together constitute the decision environment. Along each vector lie activities and expertise that merit investment in order to achieve business goals.

Balanced vectors that retain the basic plane topology indicate a coherent, scalable and effective decision support architecture (see Figure 2b). Coordinated progress across all five vectors or dimensions would clearly contribute to improved financial performance on a risk-adjusted basis. In this case the relative contributions in each dimension reinforce and improve the processes and decisions in the other dimensions.

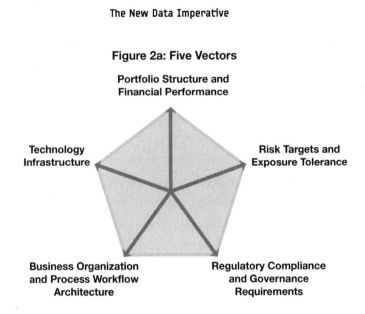

Figure 2a: Five Vectors

The decisions and processes that support business objectives can be categorized into five dimensions in a frame of reference; each dimension maps into a specific domain of expertise and business function.

Unbalanced vectors indicate limitations on the business because of shortcomings in one or more functional areas, which are thus highlighted for improvement via organizational and/or infrastructure investments. The skewed vectors in Figure 2c show that both portfolio structure and risk-taking have moved beyond the capabilities of the other three dimensions and that decisions along the five dimensions are likely being made at different temporal scales.

This distortion currently affects the entire capital markets industry and reflects the stress faced by both internal governance at major money center institutions and regulators globally.

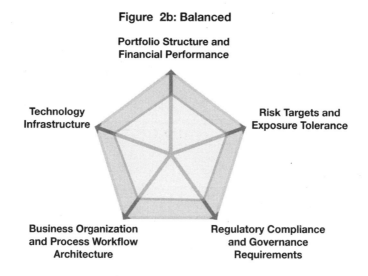

Figure 2b: Balanced

Portfolio Structure and Financial Performance

Technology Infrastructure

Risk Targets and Exposure Tolerance

Business Organization and Process Workflow Architecture

Regulatory Compliance and Governance Requirements

A balanced business architecture where all processes and decision support systems are scaling to meet expanding and changing requirements will retain the topology of the star-shaped reference structure. The capabilities along each dimension will increase proportionately as the demand from the evolution portfolio and financial performance decisions generate additional load.

From what we now know it's obvious that risk management processes and technology failed industrywide during the subprime meltdown. Technology alone will not solve the current crisis and prevent the next one. But as noted earlier, technology empowers the expert to perform more efficiently, and improved technology becomes ever more necessary as both financial instruments and trading strategies become more complex and global.

Figure 3 illustrates how complex capital markets operations have become, showing the domains across the front office,

Figure 2c: Unbalanced

Portfolio Structure and Financial Performance

Technology Infrastructure

Risk Targets and Exposure Tolerance

Business Organization and Process Workflow Architecture

Regulatory Compliance and Governance Requirements

The topology is skewed in this unbalanced business architecture in which some of the processes and decision support systems are not scaling possibly due to underinvestment or unanticipated changes in requirements. The result is that more investment funds will be tied up in corrective or remedial measures than in business improvement.

middle office and back office where market data is captured and used to generate new information to support business goals.

The financial crisis exposed the vulnerability that has arisen as a feeds and speeds explosion has hit existing infrastructures. The remedy is to start thinking very differently about designing the infrastructure for front office and middle office; the next-generation infrastructure should be based on the paradigm of a shared platform that will service both front and middle office. The design goal should be a new information management architecture that will make it possible to build, sustain and dynamically manage the chain that transforms data into information and insight. Only this will, in turn, enable decision making that produces positive risk adjusted returns.

The path to rebalance the vectors is to enhance each dimension to improve the transformation of data to actionable insight and effective decisions (data → information → insight → decision). Table 2 indicates the sections of the decision cycle that would benefit from investment in a particular dimension.

The disparity in IT infrastructure capabilities and emerging business requirements is a perhaps inevitable consequence of the recent explosion in both data volumes and rates of data flows. The shift to riskier assets in securitization and trading has increased that disparity and stressed IT infrastructures even further. Assuming this trend continues after what some are calling the Great Recession, the acute need for a new architecture design optimized for information flows will persist. Financial institutions will face increasing competitive pressure to invest in an infrastructure that can reliably transform data into action-

Table 2: Enhancing Dimensional Vectors

Dimensions	Data	Information	Insight	Decision
Portfolio structure	X	X	X	X
Risk targets	X	X	X	X
Regulatory and internal compliance		X	X	X
Business process architecture	X	X	X	
Technology infrastructure	X	X	X	X

Figure 3: Front Office to Back Office

Front Office	
Trading	
Pricing	Prop Trading
Client Dealing	Trade Execution
Market/Reference Data Integration	
Sales	
Planning & Coverage	Relationship Mgmt.
Capital Markets	
Corporate Finance	M&A
Securitization	

Mid Office	
Trade Support	
Portfolio Mgmt.	Product Control
Product Development	Performance Mgmt.
Historical Data	Transaction History (LCM)
Risk	
Market Risk	Credit Risk
Operational Risk	Risk Reporting
Liquidity & ALM	Econ. Capital Mgmt.
Collateral Management	Counterparty Risk

Back Office	
Common	
Credit Admin.	Custody Services
Corp. Actions & Dividends	Fails Handling
P&L & Client Reporting	Payments
CRM	Tax Accounting
Clearing & Settlements	
FX & Money Market	OTC & Struct. Prod.
Securities & Repos	Commodities

Supervision	
Strategy	
Business Strategy	Planning
MIS	Marketing
Strategy	
Bus. & IT Architecture	Service Level Mgmt.
Finance	
Fin. Account. & Reporting	Fin. Analysis & Control
Compliance	
Internal Audit	Regulatory Compliance

Business functions and domains that make up the front, middle, and back office and the supervisory/governance functions are part of the information flow. The availability of the same data and derived data to all decisions makers across these domains is critical for business goals.

able information and insight. Specifically, the required capabilities will include:

- Capturing and operating on live market data for real-time portfolio and balance sheet decisions
- Integrating real-time, historical and reference data to present a single view of truth to various user communities
- Managing the flow of data from various sources to support decision and reporting workflows off a shared service platform

Today's market turbulence and measures to offset it intensify the focus on these and other specific technology challenges such as counterparty risk management and the increased compliance burden expected in a more heavily regulated industry. Capital markets firms increasingly require systems that provide intraday risk management across asset classes, trading desks and departments, and data management software that regularizes data for risk modeling. As these requirements shape demand for new technology and help direct investment funds to new solutions, the vendor and research community is taking note. The key characteristics of the next generation of IT solutions are emerging. We will cover these trends in the remainder of the book.

Chapter 2

How We Got to Where We Are

SINCE 2006 the global economy has been experiencing slowing growth and increasing volatility in asset prices, and we have recently seen a near complete breakdown of the checks and balances built into the global financial system since World War II. At this point it is still unclear when and how the recovery will begin. However, the global system is at a juncture where major structural reforms are clearly needed before progress can be made. In an economy, financial markets intermediate the capital flows and allocation of investment pools seeking a predictable risk-adjusted return, and currently neither the projections of returns nor the evaluations of risks to capital are predictable. It would be instructive to review how we got to this state of affairs before we focus on the elements that will form the path to recovery.

The mission of institutions in financial markets can be summarized in three interrelated objectives:

- Allocate investment capital
- Manage the risk to capital in an optimized way
- Service and retain customers

Sell-side institutions raise capital and create and sell securities to investors to finance economic activity. Over time, new investment products such as derivatives (options, asset-backed securities, securitized loans, etc.) have been designed to mitigate various types of risk and cater to investors' differing return/risk tolerances. Derivatives were developed to enable distribution of risk to those best equipped to assume specific types of risk, thus eliminating extreme concentrations of risk in one or a few firms, or in certain asset classes. Beginning in the early 1990s, the number of derivative instruments proliferated to provide risk mitigation for more complex credit- and asset-backed securities at more granular levels. As derivatives are traded at multiple venues, the transaction volumes and frequency of pre-trade analytical operations in real time increase dramatically. As a result, the information that must be maintained online to support a diverse array of user applications grows exponentially.

With the transition to decimalization in securities pricing in the last decade, the possible price points between two point values increased by orders of magnitude, and the baseline data volume for complete price and quote histories exploded. However, the need for retaining all granular data was not immediately apparent. As the use of quantitative models and algorithmic trading spread, this granular data became critical to understanding historical price trends and volatility. Retaining granular data for pre-trade and post-trade analytics, as well as quantitative strategy development, in turn heightened the demand for very large volume, online information repositories.

The globalization of trading, increases in the number of trading venues and the cross-listing of shares on multiple exchanges all significantly raise the volume of high-value data that needs to be available for trading, portfolio and risk management decisions. The shift to model-based trading and risk analytics also increases the frequency of access and data consumption of a diverse user community. As an extension of this trend, electronic/program trading evolved into algorithmic trading in the late 1990s. This is now rapidly emerging as a dominant trading strategy (see Table 1).

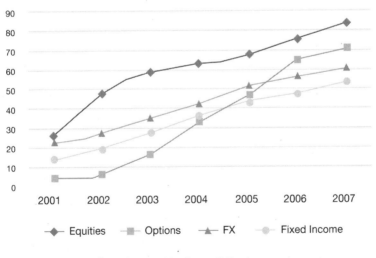

Table 1: Electronic Trading Adoption Across Asset Classes

Source: Aite Group Estimate

In relation to trading capacity, quote and message volumes have surged as a result of decimalization (see Table 2). In addition, electronic communication networks (ECNs) and the ability to route orders to multiple trading platforms have led to a decrease in average trade execution size, as institutional investors exploit effective means for executing large blocks of stock without perturbing market behavior.

Portfolio and trading decisions are being automated faster and rely on sophisticated quantitative models that incorporate real-time market data into the algorithmic processes. The capture rate of the data and the latency with which it is used in the application systems have become key differentiators in deter-

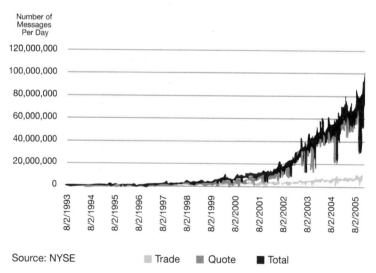

Table 2: Growth in Message Rates

NYSE TAQ Data

mining profitability at the trading desk. Price arbitrage opportunities exist for only small fractions of a second. During these short periods the fastest and most agile market players have a narrow window to secure the best prices across multiple trading venues and thus avoid less profitable trades. Reducing the latency between a market data event and submitting an order or providing a quote has become a key competitive advantage. Both proprietary traders and buy-side clients rely on fast access to markets to help them win the game. Low latency also helps traders mitigate risks by allowing them to unwind positions and pull quotes off the market before they are exploited by others as market conditions change.

In addition, regulatory initiatives such as Regulation NMS (National Market System) in the United States and MiFID (Markets in Financial Instruments Directive) in the United Kingdom are causing market fragmentation. One consequence is exploding amounts of market data that must be captured and processed in real time. Furthermore, frequency of trade order at declining average order sizes is also rising. To give an example of what this all means, the daily rate of quotes on U.S. listed securities recently rose by 250 percent.

In this environment, profits depend on rapid decisions about whether to trade based upon the ability to monitor market dynamics and the impact on portfolio positions. In addition, changes in market structure are opening the playing field to new exchanges and multilateral trading platforms, even as they drive down latency for transactions from milliseconds to hundreds of microseconds.

The growth in messages on Wall Street, from 120,000 per minute in June 2005 to 907,000 per minute in June 2008,[1] creates a pressing need for enterprises to search speedily and accurately through these unending and ever-expanding data avalanches to perform mission-critical business analysis or meet demands for legal or regulatory compliance. Message growth rises with the frequency and volume of trading. On Wall Street the average number of trades a day has increased from about 5 million in January 2000 to 25 million in January 2008. Today, Wall Street is dealing with more than 400 million traded shares a day, 150 million shares more a day than in 2000.[2]

These developments in capital markets have driven innovations in technology for real-time data streaming, execution models for running queries continuously against live data, and the ability to correlate real-time data, historical trend data and reference data. "For traders the real challenge is to make sense of this fire-hose of information that is squirting at them," Brian Traquair, president of capital markets and banking systems company Sungard, told the Financial Times in 2008, indicating that they need more memory in their computers and faster systems that can compensate for interruptions in the data flow. This has meant addressing performance issues to enable tens of thousands of messages per second per server, with processing latency measured in milliseconds. Clustered models have also been developed for streaming data to improve reliability and provide high availability and thus meet critical enterprise requirements.

Low latency has traditionally been very expensive to achieve. Network infrastructure and wide area links in particular have been costly to set up and operate, leading to sharing of resources; building a dedicated solution for low-latency trading was possible only for the major players. However, this has changed in recent years, and taking an end-to-end view of all the components of the trading platform and market data can deliver both cost savings and lower latency. Low latency is no longer limited to the largest players.

By exploiting low-cost hardware, the ever-decreasing cost of network connectivity and prepackaged software solutions, cost-effective market data and hosting services can be used to transform the economics of low-latency trading platforms. Although significant investment may still be necessary, an efficient trading infrastructure with consistently low and reliable latency will enable traders to exploit rapidly changing market conditions. With estimates suggesting that a one-millisecond improvement in latency could be worth up to $100 million a year to a large investment bank, the size of the prize should not be underestimated. Not surprisingly, the industry as a whole is moving toward lower latency.

As the financial services industry tunes its risk management operations to eliminate the weaknesses exposed by the credit crisis, new regulations may significantly increase official scrutiny of business operations. Adding impetus to this and other likely moves is a new perception that measuring risk is more complex than previously thought. For this reason tighter regulatory reporting requirements and a deeper granular level of detail can be expected. Among the other changes we think we'll see is the need for companies to detail financial results by product line or business unit. This in turn will generate new requirements for the IT organization to manage earlier information availability and flow to decision support systems.

Organizations might be able to accelerate processes to address latency, but that doesn't necessarily mean that they will be able to do all the right things faster. The growth of trading data alone—according to one estimate, the volume of market data messages will soar from under 4 billion messages per day in 2006 to nearly 130 billion per day by 2010—is putting a major stress on system capabilities.[3]

In addition, the biggest problem for risk groups is that they don't have the systems to evaluate large exposures when banks make very large investments. This can lead to huge losses if the risk is not analyzed. Large exposure could result from changes in market variables, such as interest rates, or from counterparty risk. When banks take big positions, as in foreign exchange markets, real-time risk management should indicate when they should hedge their positions. Banks, moreover, need to examine the risk of investing in different securities and how the different securities are tied to each other. If one business unit of the bank has a large position in IBM equities, for instance, and another unit has a position in IBM bonds, the two positions need to be evaluated in tandem.

Thus, the recent changes in capital markets—with new ones expected in 2009 and beyond—will require trades and investments to be processed more rapidly and accurately than ever before. Coupled with this is the need to do risk analysis as rapidly as data on trading and investment positions is compiled.

Historically, innovations in information and communications technology that have improved crisis resolution mechanisms have been a key driver of global productivity growth. This is borne out by the analysis of post–World War II financial crises by economists Carmen Reinhart and Kenneth S. Rogoff, cited in chapter 1. "Multifactor productivity," which includes technological change and spontaneous organizational and production improvements, more than doubled its contribution to the gross domestic product in the United States between 1995–2004, compared with 1980–1995.[4] As a new Wall Street takes shape, the question is whether technology, in the form of risk control and analytics, can hasten the process.

As professors Reinhart and Rogoff show, a key element in every recovery has been finding better ways to turn incomplete, confusing information about new financial risks into profitable knowledge. For today's capital markets firms, the focus must also be on making market information and trading knowledge available and visible to decision makers far sooner than they have been.

As noted in chapter 1, IOSCO identified inadequate technological resources as being at least partly responsible for the subprime crisis. Clearly, the people making decisions about portfolio risks and balance sheet integrity need the best tools they can get. However, they also need the insight and judgment that accumulated experience, historical perspective, intellect and professional discipline provide. The human dimension to restoring and preserving the integrity of the markets cannot be forgotten. Ron Papanek, head of hedge fund business in New

York–based risk management systems provider RiskMetrics Group, drew attention to this aspect of financial engineering when he said, "Technology allows for the expert to perform more efficiently, and becomes even more necessary as instruments become more complex. You still need the experts, and have to have discipline in the management of monitoring risk. Technology will facilitate it, but a lot of people expect it to solve the problem. It's just a tool."[5]

The New Trading Platform: Technology Enabling the Evolution

Although getting the most out of a tool depends on the wisdom and skill with which it is used, technological innovations will continue to fuel the development of the U.S. capital markets. Just around the corner, for example, are fourth-generation "hedging algorithms" that automate trading in multiple instruments simultaneously to hedge risk. Although this type of trading occurs today, it is a complicated process involving multiple steps and different people.

As a result of cross-asset portfolio trading, other changes are also taking place. The equity and equity option markets are a good example. The equity exchanges have entered into the options arena with NYSE's purchase of Arca Options and NASDAQ's creation of its own options exchange. Consequently, over the next three to five years this transformation will fuel demands for new technology that accommodates access to these multiple venues and provides higher levels of agility to deal with the ever-increasing volumes (see Table 3).

Share-trading volumes have remained high even in the pro-
longed bear market, but at lower unit prices requiring more
trading volatility to achieve desired profit margins. As a consequence, investors and financial institutions are challenged to
more closely control costs, speed operations, consider more
factors in every decision and make use of information from a
variety of sources to instantaneously assess exposure to risk and
to identify lower-risk, higher-margin opportunities.

Newer risk-related financial engineering tools can provide
greater accuracy and quality in processing large amounts of
information. These tools may deal with extremely complex
transactions such as managing hedge funds, tracking derivatives
trading across asset categories and analyzing program trading
patterns and results. Regulation is another strong force that
drives risk management approaches toward these new technologies and solutions. Legislation such as the Sarbanes-Oxley
Act of 2002 and stringent internal trading/risk controls have
mandated a higher priority for risk assessment and timely
reporting of risk, both of which require reliable and instantaneous access to risk-related information.

Compliance with regulatory requirements is not a new element for capital markets companies. But as we have already suggested, there will likely be a new wave of financial sector
regulatory changes. One reason for this is that inconsistency in
the way the regulations are applied has emerged as an important
issue. Commercial banks, for example, are much more closely
regulated and supervised than investment banks and other
financial institutions. Writing in the Financial Times in Jan.

Table 3: U.S. Equity Options Growth
1995-2008 YTD*
(000s of contracts)

Source: OCC
*Data through 5/30/08

2009, Ilian Mihov, an economics professor at Insead, observed, "The fact that some entities are closely regulated but others are not is a big part of the problem" in resolving the financial crisis. Accordingly, there have been calls from many quarters for extending more stringent regulations to more of the world's financial institutions.

Even apart from this, the impact of regulations and compliance requirements on business processes and IT systems has already grown substantially for two reasons. First, as capital markets firms have evolved to do business on a truly global scale and participate directly in financial markets around the world, they have come under the scrutiny of an increasing number of regulatory bodies. Second, the reports needed to prove compliance have indeed become complex in all aspects: time periods to be covered, variety of audits to be performed and also the number of integrated reports that cross multiple IT systems and databases.

This is the legacy of a system that dates back more than a century. Over time it has had new pieces grafted onto it because of financial meltdowns, innovations and other events. The result is a multilayered patchwork rather than a more efficient market regulatory system.

Creating a Data Strategy for Regulatory Compliance and Risk Management

Compliance in its very simplest form consists of two components: the processes and methods that ensure compliance and the reports that validate that a firm has complied with the regulatory requirements. From a data architecture perspective, the impact has traditionally been felt more on the creation and delivery of the validation reports. But increasingly the compliance requirements to prevent violations before they happen, such as in antimoney laundering (AML), impose new requirements on data architectures.

The first challenge in dealing with compliance for capital markets companies is the lack of coordination among various internal and external regulatory bodies. Also, within a company reports needed to validate compliance must be able to access data from multiple systems. But not all systems have consistent data formats, consistent data or equivalent levels of data granularity.

Compliance regulations touch various operational aspects of a financial institution including but not limited to financial reporting, AML, privacy, customer communication, capital adequacy and operational risk. The various regulatory agencies stipulate requirements in one or several of these areas, as shown in Table 4.[6]

Add to these difficulties of ensuring compliance the fact that various regulations require different levels of information granularity and even different terminologies. Each of these additional factors has the potential to introduce inconsistencies. Encouragingly, the various regulatory bodies are taking positive steps to converge and move toward consistency. In the meantime, since regulatory differences do exist and probably will persist at least to some degree, it is necessary to have an integrated strategy and architecture to meet compliance issues effectively.

As noted, compliance affects IT systems and architecture in many respects. Chapman, Josefowicz, Walsh and Grossman[7] articulate the main and common threads of the regulations as they impact IT systems dealing with:

- Data and network security
- Data integrity
- Record retention
- Business processes and policies

Data and network security issues must ensure that there is no internal or external tampering with data sources and applica-

Table 4: Compliance and Regulations

Compliance Issue Types	Examples of Corresponding Regulations
Privacy	• Gramm-Leach-Bliley Act (United States) • Insurance Conduct of Business Rules (Europe) • Anti Money Laundering Directive (United States) • Proceeds of Crime Act (United Kingdom)
AML	• Patriot Act (United States) • Anti Money Laundering Directive (United States) • Proceeds of Crime Act (United Kingdom)
Customer communication	• Insurance Mediation Directive (Europe) • Gramm-Leach-Bliley Act (United States)
Financial reporting	• Sarbanes-Oxley Act (United States) • International Financial Reporting Standards incorporating the International Accounting Standards (IFRS/IAS) • Financial Services Authority Prudential Source Book (United Kingdom)
Capital adequacy	• Basel II (International) • IFRS/IAS • Solvency II (European Union)
Operational risk	• Basel II (International) • IFRS/IAS • Solvency II (European Union)

tions. Data integrity deals with data quality and consistency across the various disparate application and data sources. This is essential for reliable reporting that validates adherence to compliance requirements. Record retention deals with retention policies, actual storage and access to historical data. With respect to IT, business processes and policies deal with the ability to document and model processes, workflows and services. Table 5 details the impact of various compliance components on IT systems and environments.

Table 5: Impact of Compliance on IT

	Data and Network Security	Data and Information Integrity	Policies, Procedures, and Processes	Record Retention and Accessibility
Privacy	X	X		X
AML		X		X
Customer communication		X	X	X
Financial reporting	X	X	X	X
Capital adequacy	X	X	X	
Operational risk	X		X	X

There is little argument about the objectives of compliance among business groups such as general managers, chief financial officers, auditors and IT. However, as Rebecca Graves pointed out in DM Review in Sept. 2005, they may have similar issues but very different perspectives when they begin to break down the aspects of compliance. The business focuses on the process, workflow and procedures, whereas IT focuses on the technology aspects of compliance.

The business side tends to focus on the integrity and accuracy of information, access to information, procedures that facilitate compliance, proper audit and document trails, adaptability to change and adequate controls when changes are implemented. IT administrators focus on data integrity among distributed systems, preventing unauthorized access and tampering with all aspects of the systems environment, providing real-time access to data 24/7 and ensuring that the compliance requirements are met in a timely fashion.

Thus the data and overall system architecture must provide a host of capabilities to meet compliance requirements. These capabilities include access control, auditing, integration and aggregation, analytics, policy definition and implementation, monitoring, data disposition and destruction, process registry and documentation, metadata, workflow, data quality, real-time access and delivery.

Various organizations typically are at different stages of maturity with respect to fulfilling compliance requirements in a systemic and enterprisewide manner. Table 6 summarizes the typical environment as a company marches along the maturity continuum.

In summary, as regulatory requirements become more stringent and more intensive, a comprehensive data architecture must not only meet the requirements effectively but leverage the investment into value within the broader business strategy. To deal with all this, and more, companies need a data strategy.

A data strategy is about identifying what people need to make real-time decisions. It establishes the frequency—intraday, perhaps, or hourly—with which new data comes in, and how it's stored and made accessible to users in real or near real time. It's the architecture for a sustained, continuous flow of data to the consuming applications in an environment where high-frequency and high-speed execution are essential to give a complete perspective of what is going on in the markets.

A data strategy is also the basis of an adequate risk platform for the chief risk officer (CRO) and management team to use to assess risk management across the enterprise. With it the CRO and management team will be able to assess the

**Table 6: From Early to Mature Stages in
Establishing Compliant Systems**

	Early Stage	Mature Stage
Overall Objective	Penalty avoidance	Integrated into the broad business strategy
Use of IT Systems	Minimal	Extensive
Implementation	Individual business units or compliances	Broad enterprisewide framework to meet compliance requirements
Data Architecture	Siloed	Enterprisewide
Timeliness	Batch-centric	Real-time
Reporting	From individual operational data stores	Enterprise data warehouse and data marts
Metadata	Nonexistent	Metadata an integral component of framework
Data Integrity	Separate process	Integrated into the framework

concentration of risk and be empowered to overrule individual trading desks.

As things are, however, existing systems designed to service different business units do not provide the CRO with the appropriate risk infrastructure. Re-engineering risk platforms is a first step. The second is designing the infrastructure so that as the business grows the data strategy naturally expands with it.

Chapter 3

Data Architecture for the Future

TO A SIGNIFICANT DEGREE, it was the failure of risk management that brought the capital markets system into jeopardy and forced government intervention to prevent a collapse of the entire financial services industry.

To analyze risk accurately, trading desks need to collect relevant data from different in-house databases and external sources of live data in a timely manner. Generally, risk management practice has been satisfied with receiving data from trading systems a day later (T+1), however, this is no longer acceptable due to both the acceleration of trading cycles and the complexity of instruments involved. The real-time (or intraday) visibility to changing risk factors and evaluation of balance sheet exposure has become critical. The inability of existing infrastructure to provide this level of visibility and monitoring capability is where many firms, and the capital markets as a whole, stumbled. "Some big banks failed to keep track of the risks as the volumes built up," Nigel Woodward, Intel's London-based director of financial services, told the Financial Times.[1] If for example a bank bought a collateralized debt obligation (CDO) in a subprime mortgage without recording and tracking the instrument to a residential property in Texas, Woodward explained, the bank might already have had a full exposure to the Texas property without knowing it. In such a case—and it was far from isolated—the bank's capacity to measure risk couldn't match the system's ability to handle the CDO.

Such situations where all relevant data cannot be integrated into the data set that is used in risk mitigation can be avoided by designing systems for transparent data flow at every point in the process—from pricing a trade to risk analysis to getting information by asset class and then managing the economic capital of the company. With a data strategy directed to real-time integration of data into actionable information, the architecture can be drawn to sustain a continuous flow of data to consuming applications. In an environment where high-frequency, high-speed execution is critical for portfolio decisions, a risk management infrastructure designed to optimize information flow in real time and to integrate historical and live market data enables the chief risk officer and the management team to assess risk concentrations and balance sheet exposure proactively.

In most firms it takes data from various systems at least a day to reach decision makers for post-trade analysis and reporting (see Figure 1).

Figure 1: Data Flow – Current State

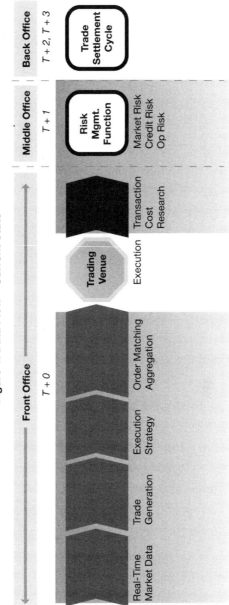

Front Office

Middle Office

Back Office

T + 0

T + 1

T + 2, T + 3

Real-Time Market Data

Trade Generation

Execution Strategy

Order Matching Aggregation

Trading Venue

Execution

Transaction Cost Research

Risk Mgmt. Function

Market Risk
Credit Risk
Op Risk

Trade Settlement Cycle

The disparity in data capture rates at the front office, which consumes real-time data, and the schedule with which that data in aggregated, cleansed form is delivered to the middle office, which uses longer-range trend data in decision making, may often have adverse consequences for managing firmwide risk and economic capital.

The front office acts on real-time market data and trade transactions that are fed from trade order and execution management systems using approved models and strategies. In a typically single-asset trading environment, the visibility to exposures built across different portfolios across different desks is limited; correlation data on prices and volatilities may not reflect current state and may even be several days old. The middle office, generally engaged in post-trade processing and reporting (e.g., P&L monitoring, position management, risk analytics), relies on aggregated data and historical trend data; in some respects it may be working on day-old data and for some analyses relies on weekly and monthly updates. Full portfolio valuations are still biweekly (or monthly) events in most large organizations (see Figure 2).

For both front office and middle office users, actionable information requires contextual presentation of data from multiple channels and must be presented with the related background and with reference to linkages between related markets. Time lags in data delivery from some sources and failure to update referential links can easily distort decision making. To avoid this the supervisory processes that oversee capital allocation and risk management must enable:

Figure 2: Two Views of "Truth"

Front Office	Middle Office
Algorithmic trading, quantitative analysis, post-trade analytics	*Credit risk and market risk management*
Need: 'Up-to-the-tick' market information and vast amounts of historical information	**Need:** Improve risk management – better access to information across product silos and market data
Issue: Cannot store large amounts of historical data due to performance limitations of traditional RDBMS or proprietary databases	**Issue:** Data latencies in receiving market data and position data from the front office

- Visibility and transparency of a continuous flow of consolidated information from all related markets, including markets where real assets are traded so that correlations in price and volatility across these markets can be identified
- Synchronization of analytical processes that tap integrated data to support portfolio decisions and balance sheet management within the same time window so that latencies in content capture do not distort a more holistic view of risks and liquidity
- Closer timing, approaching simultaneity, of asset pricing and risk pricing at the portfolio level and in the pre-trade decision cycle

As the business structure of the industry changes, both the business process architecture and technology architecture also need to change. Advanced technology will provide some of the answers, and taking control of information flow from many sources into critical decision processes is an essential step. One key requirement for firms in the capital markets is the ability to get positions in real time. They don't need this for every market, but in foreign exchange, equities and structured products the requirement for real-time analytics is critical, including assessment of a bank's overall trading position.

As it stands now, most securities-trading organizations lack the capability to evaluate the shifting risk exposures of major positions in real time; such a facility would have helped avoid losses by more proactive hedging and position management. It would also enable banks to examine correlations in risk profiles among different securities (e.g., among debt securities, asset-backed instruments, convertibles of the same entity or between industry sectors).

The sheer complexity, opaqueness and systemic risk embedded in the capital markets today demand more rapid and accurate processing of trades than ever before. In addition, there is the need for risk data on trading and investment positions to be stored for compliance review and auditing requirements as an integrated database for on-demand access.

Failure to estimate their risk exposure in a timely manner cost several financial houses tens of billions of dollars each in write-downs and losses in the subprime crisis and credit crunch. Success in identifying the drivers changing current market circumstances and how new systems respond to these changes made the difference between, say, a $54.6 billion loss reported in one case in August 2008 and a second-quarter profit reported by PR Newswire of $162 million announced by T. Rowe Price in July 2008.

Design Paradigm for the Next-Generation Technology Infrastructure

Competitiveness in today's capital markets requires control of data flows and process flows to support real-time portfolio and trading decisions. A highly tuned, integrated infrastructure is essential, yet most firms are far from achieving a reasonable state of readiness to manage emerging, rapidly evolving business requirements.

Simply expressed, the frontline infrastructure now needs to:

- Accommodate high volumes of diverse data on global markets at an increasing rate
- Complete computations against short-range data and integrate real-time data with longer-term trend data across asset classes and reference data
- Consolidate and aggregate new data and existing long-term-trend data, and use the complete data set for developing quantitative models and trading and portfolio management methodologies
- Monitor and measure risk and exposure to the firm's business units and the balance sheet across asset classes

- Monitor, test and validate efficacy of models and hedging strategies
- Complete reporting cycles for internal and regulatory compliance

Financial institutions have traditionally conducted business in specialized silos (i.e., fixed income trading, equities, derivatives, etc.). However, any efficiencies of specialization are now being superseded by the linkages and interdependencies among asset classes, trading/hedging strategies for generating higher returns, potential implications in terms of balance sheet exposure and new regulatory mandates. Information now needs to flow more rapidly across the firm and be more quickly visible to decision makers. Reporting and analytical processes that extend over several days are no longer acceptable.

In terms of a next-generation architecture that enables a more unified view of the new and historical data across front and middle office, it makes sense to think of users who are characterized by their patterns of data consumption. For instance, pre-trade analytics relies on the most recent data and trade order generation uses relatively short range data (latest 10 minutes or last two hours of trades and quotes data, news feeds, etc). Risk monitoring and position management need a united view of recent history that may span several days or several months of trades, changes in credit ratings and benchmark indices and their volatilities. The data flow can be managed in three layers (analogous to lanes on a highway) where real-time data can flow unimpeded to applications that require low latency; applications that use trade transaction data will capture updates on a different layer that is higher latency but richer in content. All data is stored in a shared, disk-based repository for quantitative analysis, reporting and performance measurement. Data can be managed for high availability at the repository for all user communities within minutes (see Figure 3).

In contrast, the prevailing architecture in most firms is a consequence of the decades-old evolution of the adoption of client/server technology. If one were to imagine a circuit of data flow to the point of use, the current pathways for data to reach users would be illustrated by where the data movement is achieved by batch processes scheduled over many hours and/or through traditional messaging systems over the network. The figure also illustrates the specialized, dedicated databases that have been developed to enable autonomy and agility for functional areas and business units. However, the constraints of the existing environment become clear when the volumes and flow rates rise across these fragmented databases and when portfolio and trading decisions, as well as supervisory controls, require access to a more complete view of interrelated data. Adding capacity by increasing available physical resources will not solve the problem entirely, especially when the infrastructure is stressed by the speed of data flow and the volumes that need to be accessed and analyzed in real time or near real time (see Figure 4).

To remedy these limitations and mitigate operational risks, organizations are exploring paths to enhancing and/or replacing the existing infrastructure. These new systems need to meet the following fundamental criteria in order to justify the investment

Figure 3: Three Layer Stack

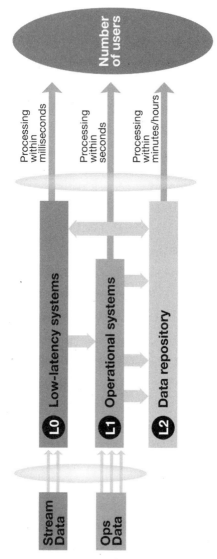

Transformation of the horizontal data flow to a three layer stack to manage information.

Figure 4: Cycle of Silos

Problem: specialized systems create
data silos, add latency.

and account for the operational and technological risks of the
upgrade:

- Performance that results in low latency to make real-
  time data available (in subseconds) to applications that
  need the latest state-of-the-order book, quotes and interactions with trade execution venues. Low latency applies
  not only to the capture of live data from external sources

but also to the presentation of data for queries and computations to applications used in trade pricing, risk analysis, order generation, execution strategy and compliance reporting

- Improved throughput to persist in capturing real-time data from several sources at rates of hundreds of thousands to millions of messages a second. The data may include market trade and quote data for several types of securities, corporate events and updates to reference data from internal sources
- Continuous aggregation and distribution of input data and derived data and report generation

Furthermore, the complexity and heterogeneity of the infrastructure implied by the diagram in Figure 4 should be reduced significantly. In a real-time decision-support environment, data flow workloads and heavy computational workloads inevitably are coupled with and overlap one another. Optimal performance will require a more homogeneous architecture that allows for design and implementation of workloads that serve different user needs and must be run concurrently.

Information as a Continuous Process Flow Across the Firm

Organizations need an information-processing architecture that can treat the flow of information as a continuous process with tight coupling between data flow on various instruments and decision events that include sophisticated analytics and reporting for a variety of user communities. Higher speed and/or increased volume at any point in the flow must be accommodated by scalability and speed downstream. By one estimate, for every trade transaction on equities and equity derivatives there are over 5,000 quotes. A time series of quotes leading to a transaction at a point in time indicates liquidity flow and is more meaningful if the quotes are collected from multiple venues. It is possible to map a path to the trade price through the quotes, and this provides valuable insight into the structure of information generated by trading activity.

As noted previously, trading structured products for higher returns has become the norm, and hedging strategies using different asset classes are employed for leverage and risk mitigation. The autonomy, flexibility and specialization within trading desks of the past no longer work in this environment. Cross-asset trading and hedging are simply not possible in firms with siloed data and processes. When equity trades are hedged using futures, for instance, such applications as pre-trade analytics, pricing-to-order generation and transaction cost analysis depend on access to data from both the equity markets and the futures markets. In addition, the presentation of information should include referential information such as updated yield curves and benchmark index data, and should deliver the complete set as close to the application as possible. Similarly, mortgage-backed asset-trading applications need a view of the security prices, loan portfolio pricing and residential real estate valuations. The transparency and visibility requirement is determined by whichever data flow has the highest update frequency.

Supervisory control processes (such as risk and compliance monitoring) on the trading cycle (automated or not) should not depend on the scheduled delivery (such as batch movement of data across silos) of raw and derived data.

OTC processing is one example that suffers from desynchronized movement of data. Infrastructure that was developed when agility was prized is under stress—partly due to MiFID requirements and partly due to increased use of these instruments by the buy-side. The attribution and settlement processes are nearing breaking point.

The new mantra is no surprise along the trade life cycle. The auditing requirements under MiFID and Regulation NMS (Reg NMS) will force firms to produce an audit trail of pricing and valuations as well as order management and trade execution procedures.

The key features of the new generation infrastructure are:

- Continuous flow of real-time market data from multiple sources into applications that need to act on market price and volatility data
- Continuous flow of information from trading systems into post-trade processes and risk and compliance monitoring systems
- Persistence of real-time and trade transaction data in a data store that also hosts reference data and analytical data (historical trend data and results)
- Support for scalability with respect to concurrent applica-

tions, data volume and inbound data sources and capture rates
- Support for data models and data architecture that allow homogeneous presentation of information to reporting applications

The design should enable construction of workflows over the data flow in order to support trading and portfolio decisions (see Figure 5).

The Increased Emphasis on Real-time Risk Analysis

Many banks are adopting real-time risk and financial reporting capabilities based upon a core risk-analysis engine tied to all parts of their business. This is a major change in capital markets.

Whereas enterprise risk management was an adjunct to a bank's operations until recently, most banks now view it as essential. This change puts the risk analytics for banking at the center of all functional operations and links the front, middle and back offices (see Figure 6).

As a consequence, according to the Algo Research Quarterly, the bank of the future will very likely rely upon a "unified platform [that] operates within a standard framework for risk management that encompasses market, credit, liquidity and operational risk, as well as asset and liability management" and "provides the foundation for true enterprise-wide management of profitability and risk capital."

Figure 5: Shared Services

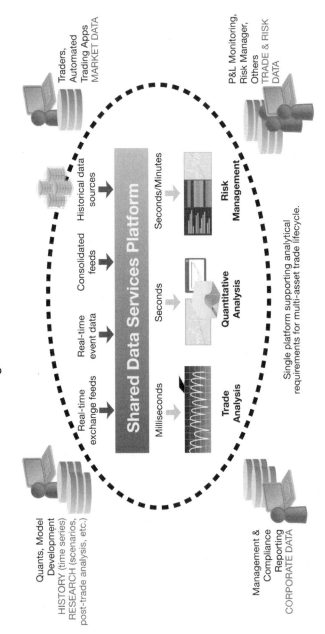

Traders, Automated Trading Apps
MARKET DATA

P&L Monitoring, Risk Manager, Others
TRADE & RISK DATA

Quants, Model Development
HISTORY (time series)
RESEARCH (scenarios, post-trade analysis, etc.)

Management & Compliance Reporting
CORPORATE DATA

Historical data sources

Consolidated feeds

Real-time event data

Real-time exchange feeds

Shared Data Services Platform

Seconds/Minutes

Seconds

Milliseconds

Risk Management

Quantitative Analysis

Trade Analysis

Single platform supporting analytical requirements for multi-asset trade lifecycle.

Figure 6: Bank of the Future

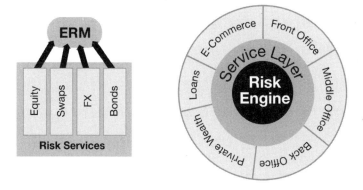

Bank of Today   **Bank of the Future**

Where enterprise risk management (ERM) is an adjunct
to the bank's operations today, tomorrow it will be at
the core, powered by a consistent analytical engine.

Shortened Latency and the Use of Complex Event-Processing Engines

Creating first-trader advantages is worth a great deal to financial institutions. One market participant using hundreds of thousands of CPUs to "create and price differentiated products, calculate value at risk and perform other risk analyses quickly" estimated that a savings of "one millisecond of latency over the course of the year ... could translate into $100 million in value"[2] for them.

To keep up with the growth in data flows, latency issues and the pressure to make rapid decisions, financial firms have adopted complex event-processing (CEP) engines that are usually linked to a messaging bus. For the typical Wall Street firm, this changes the stack to one built around a CEP engine and a message bus with suitable adapters, service brokers and monitoring.

CEP technology is a comparatively recent method of gathering intelligence from events in real time related to specific conditions or rising new patterns. Developers use it to apply sophisticated tools for defining the processing and analyzing of events, such as incoming messages. CEP enables event-driven architecture to provide the resources to assimilate, assemble, interrelate and analyze messages, creating new high-level messages that can set off a response and produce information showing exposure to risk, for example. It allows users to determine the logic to apply to messages to:

- Correlate data from multiple sources, deriving streams of information that are richer and more complete
- Compute information specifically designed to enable decisions to be made quickly
- Identify patterns or specific circumstances to enable responses to be made instantly
- Provide a big-picture view of information such as summaries, statistics and trends, or the net effect of numerous incoming events or messages
- Constantly recompute key operating values based upon complex analysis of incoming events
- Gather raw and/or result data into a database for historical analysis and/or compliance

Market players face a growing number of price-setting entities that are also sources of liquidity, and the complexities make it necessary to analyze all the opportunities. By a recent count, these price-setting entities comprise 47 so-called dark pools, three major exchanges, six regional exchanges, three ECNs and an unknown number of host dark pools, set up but not identified.[3] Hedge funds mostly use dark pools to trade large blocks of shares anonymously, sidestepping the risk of seeing the public price of a stock move on an exchange because of trading imitators.

Every trading organization's processes must identify these issues and compliance requirements and then execute effectively on the steps to deal with them. CEP solutions are particularly suited to high-volume, low-latency applications used in the capital markets and are a chief means to improve the algorithmic trading that generates an increasing share of transactions. Recent estimates suggest that almost 50 percent of all capital markets trading is now done algorithmically, and the proportion is sure to rise. As more businesses move closer to real-time operations and business processes, CEP will offer a familiar, yet powerful means for IT teams to create event-driven applications to monitor and act upon critical enterprise data-in-motion.

Chapter 4

Transforming Old to New

ONE OF THE main lessons of the current financial crisis is that major risk events are usually the consequence not of a single risk, but of converging, interrelated risks. In this as in past financial crises, most companies managed risk by silos, or by enterprise risk management programs that were enterprisewide in name only. For example, AIG considered credit default risk to manage its credit derivatives business, according to a Wall Street Journal report, but not the implication of mark-to-market accounting or liquidity risk.

It is now almost a given that companies in the financial services industry must implement enterprisewide risk management to analyze multirisk scenarios with significant potential impact on their solvency. For banks, this means integrating the analysis of credit, market and liquidity risks. For insurance companies, it means integrating investment strategy, asset liability management and balance sheet risk analysis. For all companies, critical interdependencies necessitate integrating risk management across business, financial and operational functions.

The mortgage and derivative related losses of 2007 and after were clearly compounded by inadequate risk management and accounting practices. The result shrank the assets of banks and other lenders by a staggering $2 trillion as of early 2009. This represents a cut in U.S. annual economic growth, as measured by gross domestic product, of 1.5 percent.

Banks and other highly leveraged financial institutions will bear about half of a total loss estimated to be more than $850 billion. These institutions hold equity and other capital of just 4 to 10 percent of their total assets. Thus for every dollar lost and not replaced with new capital, they will have to shrink their balance sheets by $10 to $25. This means forgoing lending or selling securities. The limits on lending and securities trading are exacerbated by the fact that current risk management practices call for banks not merely to maintain a steady capital-to-asset ratio, but to raise their capital-to-asset ratios when markets turn volatile.

"The interaction of marking assets to their market prices and the risk management practices of levered financial institutions" amplifies the impact of the initial losses, David Greenlaw of Morgan Stanley, Jan Hatzius of Goldman Sachs, Anil Kashyap of the University of Chicago and Hyun Song Shin of Princeton University said in a recent study. They noted that many institutions hold capital based on the "value at risk" of their holdings, which tends to drop when markets are calm and rise when they are volatile. Based on recent experience, they calculate such institutions on average will want to boost their capital-to-asset ratios by 5 percent because of increased risk. Even assuming that these financial institutions offset half their losses by raising $100 billion in new capital, they will still try to shrink their assets, now about $20.5 trillion, by about $2 trillion. The study concludes that the resulting limits on lending will restrain U.S. GDP growth by 1.3 percent.

As noted previously, the bank of the future will very likely rely upon a unified platform that treats risk management as a defined business discipline and encompasses market, credit, liquidity and operational risk, as well as asset and liability management. In recognition of that, companies now see implementing new risk management practices and governance as a necessary first step in shoring up their performance, satisfying regulators and winning back investors' trust.

The focus on enterprisewide risk management puts risk infrastructures in the spotlight. The single most important implication of our current economic turmoil is that robust and resilient risk management systems are vital for any organization involved in trading activity. French economics minister Christine Lagarde spoke to this point when she told reporters, "There is a risk which is operational risk, as opposed to market risk, which must be taken more seriously into consideration."

Operational risk is not just about losses related to an individual trade; it's the negative impact that inadequate risk management can have on an entire enterprise. Managing operational risk requires a support system to formalize what to do, and how to do it, when things don't work out as expected.

Not being able to manage and control operational risk leads to massive costs, and experts have warned about the failure to manage operational risk for years. Regulatory investigations, shareholder lawsuits, job terminations, earnings restatements, severe adverse publicity, loss of market capitalization, liquidity crises, volatile earnings and increased cost of capital are all areas that need to be managed and controlled. Yet the subprime mortgage meltdown and subsequent economic damage showed that only a handful of organizations had equipped themselves with robust and resilient operational risk management systems.

The key to effective operational risk management is to be able to see and understand every aspect of the business operation. This requires sufficient transparency and communication to enable decision makers to access instantaneous, accurate and actionable information across an enterprise.

Smart decisions require all business groups, including risk management, operations, finance and trading to work off the same data in real time. Many firms profess a strong commitment to risk management and streamlined data access and delivery, but the positive talk is nothing without truly optimized business processes and information flows.

An organization with information in silos cannot manage current and future operational risk effectively. Multiple, patched-together systems and individual spreadsheet applications, separated by organizational divides and interdepartmental rivalries, will defeat any attempt to manage risk across an enterprise. The complex, volatile nature of global commodity markets requires trading organizations to have a single, integrated, real-time view of all physical and derivative transactions, coupled with straight-through processing from the front office all the way to the back office.

With the right infrastructure, data is entered once at the source and all relevant parties—executives who measure performance, compliance officers, schedulers, risk managers and portfolio managers on the execution front line—get accurate information exactly when it is needed. This is what is meant by one version of the truth: it is available to all and it eliminates duplication and the potential for errors. What's more, it enables companies to set limits and control workflow by integrating across organizations and markets.

Managing risk is no longer confined to the trading desk, because it is no longer just about managing price or market risk. A mandate infringement or a regulations breach, however minor, is part of a much wider issue. Today corporate governance is paramount, requiring total transparency across the enterprise and at all levels. Any system managing operational risk must provide a complete reporting function that can transform data into actionable information.

The good news is that enterprisewide risk management can be turned to an organization's advantage. The potential benefits of enterprise risk management include positive returns, lowered cost of capital, stabilized earnings and new profit opportunities.

The Design Paradigm: To Achieve Real-time Risk Management

The current structure of IT systems lies at the heart of many of the large issues faced by capital markets firms today. Typically these systems have evolved over time to meet short-term tactical needs in a solely transactional context. This organic evolution has frequently been interrupted by mergers and acquisitions that bring together systems of different genesis and deeply scar the landscape of existing IT systems. High-profile M&A activity in recent times offered organizations the opportunity to scale in a consolidating market, gain access to the fastest-growing regions of the market and achieve critical mass in many market areas. However, the impact on operational risk was underappreciated.

The 2007 acquisition of ABN AMRO by an RBS-led consortium highlights the unprecedented complexity of the integration challenges in a major M&A event. For RBS those challenges include:

- Integrating operations in more than 50 countries (each with its own sets of regulators)
- Novating (i.e., moving from ABN AMRO to RBS plc) more than £108 billion gross of risk-weighted assets
- Evaluating more than 100,000 trading counterparties for risk and compliance
- Novating approximately 900,000 trades
- Managing approximately 2,000 integration program resources at any one time
- Consolidating and supporting more than 125 data centers and 8,000 servers

Viewed as a tool for competitiveness, IT in the capital markets can be a double-edged sword. On one hand, IT automates manual tasks for an immediate gain in productivity. On the other hand, rapid innovation in the capital markets typically outpaces IT's ability to keep up and turns past IT investment into a competitive disadvantage. Problems arise when the intrinsic rigidities of siloed operations prevent the evolution of IT infrastructure at an acceptable cost, impeding efforts to exploit new high-profit products or markets and to introduce new risk-reducing, yield-enhancing methodologies and operations.

At some point, past IT investment becomes such a liability that firms must write it off entirely and replace it with modern IT machinery. Eventually, the cycle repeats and organizations again end up in the silo syndrome.

The silo syndrome occurs in many industries, but it may be most intractable in the capital markets industry. In other industries approaches such as SOA (service-oriented architecture) have succeeded in federating past IT investment into reusable services that can be accessed on demand throughout the organization from ubiquitous Web front ends. But in the capital markets the application of the same stack of SOA technologies has been disappointing.

The result is especially disappointing because an impressive arsenal of IT solutions has been invented over the last 20 years to deal with silos across multiple industries: client/server separations, object-oriented languages, remote distributed objects, multitier technologies, distributed computing, application servers (including lighter frameworks), document-driven interaction (such as via XML), Web-based interfaces and most recently the entire promise of SOA. These innovations have helped many industries to modernize their IT infrastructures, allowing reuse of past investments in a more dynamic, real-time, STP (straight-through processing), e-commerce distributed manner that is better suited to the "just in time" operating model of many enterprises today.

In the capital markets, however, such innovations have to date failed to substantially reduce the silo syndrome. If anything, innovations have quite often become entangled with a silo, turning it into a bigger silo. Paradoxically, the innovative nature of the capital markets themselves is responsible. Financial engineering innovations, layered on top of multiple generations of prior innovations and serving as the foundation for still more innovations, have made it extremely complex for IT to model the capital markets domain. This challenge has unfortunately been obscured by the success that horizontal technology has had in other industries. That success has deluded the capital markets IT industry into trying to apply the same concepts and horizontal discourse that worked in other industries to the silo syndrome in the capital markets.

Although individual systems and applications may meet the functional needs of their primary users, when it comes to management and control functions requiring a holistic view across multiple business lines (and therefore multiple systems), such as cross-asset trade management and risk or profitability reporting, many organizations struggle to achieve a consistent, accurate and timely view of their business as a whole. An application typically presents problems to the wider business when its role changes from supporting a primary system, such as an equity derivatives trading system, to providing a businesswide service, such as a cross-asset middle office, across system boundaries and inorganic infrastructure. To counteract this, a number of capital market firms have introduced SOA platforms supplemented by message-orientated middleware (MOM) to help elevate some of the issues.

It is becoming clear, however, that technology alone is largely failing to live up to the hype of delivering better interoperability, reusability and alignment of business and technology domains. What is fundamentally required is intelligent, timely use of data, and control of the data and process flows to support real-time portfolio and trading decisions. As described below in Figure 1, data is the critical pillar in understanding operational risk and exposure.

A highly tuned, real-time integrated infrastructure is essential, yet most firms are far from achieving a reasonable state of readiness to manage emerging, rapidly evolving business requirements. As discussed in the previous chapter, the front-line infrastructure now fundamentally needs:

a. The ability to ingest high volumes of diverse data from global markets
b. The provision of aggregated views of both new and long-term data for developing quantitative models and portfolio management methodologies
c. The ability to monitor and manage risk across asset classes
d. The ability to provide back-testing of newly developed models

Figure 1: Critical Pillar

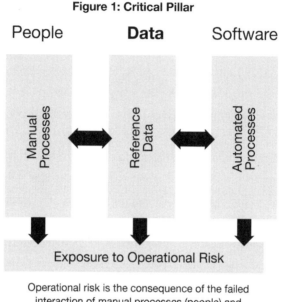

Operational risk is the consequence of the failed interaction of manual processes (people) and applications (software) with data.

In the next section we will expand upon each of these key infrastructural characteristics.

a. Ability to ingest high volumes of diverse data from global markets

The ability to access clean reference and market data from disparate sources affects the capabilities of front, middle and back office systems to monitor investment activity and manage risk. The wide range of data types being processed today encompasses reference data, such as corporate actions or instrument and client information; transaction data relating to market and deal information; and unstructured data, which supplements analysis, such as agreements and policy documents. Understanding how each of these data types is spread and used throughout the operating model is one of the first steps to obtaining the right information to tune a firm's operating infrastructure. Managing reference and market data costs an estimated $30 billion a year worldwide. At present, firms are battling against pressures to cut costs and reduce spending on IT because of dismal market conditions, while facing an increasing deluge of data volumes.

As financial institutions move to ever more sophisticated investments and counterparty risk becomes a growing concern, capital market firms need more and more data across a wider universe of content in order to research and identify areas of return or risk. To compound the situation, since the advent of MiFID and Reg NMS there have been substantial changes within capital markets concerning best execution, client classification, systematic internal IERs, pre- and post-trade transparency and the ownership of market data. These obligations have had a significant impact on providing market data, particularly in equity markets, and have led to significant growth in the volume of information generated from exchanges.

Market participants are now expected to maintain much more historical data for compliance purposes and this has boosted reference data requirements, such as revised documentation and classification data, and new types and sources of market data that had never before been published.

MiFID has also introduced greater competition into the market, as evidenced by the early success of new trading venues such as Instinet Chi-X and new market data providers such as Markit BOAT. As more trading venues enter the scene, such as Turquoise, Equiduct, BATS, NASDAQ OMX and SmartPool, the relentless rise of data volumes is set to continue. To handle soaring trade and market volumes, capital markets firms require:

- Optimized infrastructure for the storage and access of streaming and historical data
- Low-latency and high-frequency solutions that enhance the turnaround and utilization of data in the trading environment
- Capacity management processes to ensure that data flows preserve low-latency distribution within an organization and are constantly monitored and tracked
- Establishment and monitoring of average and peak thresholds in normal market conditions, with extra headroom factored in during times of unusual market conditions and high volatility
- Continuous monitoring and management of thresholds, with action taken to maintain sufficient capacity in systems and applications, networks and people prior to the resources being needed

b. The provision of aggregated views of both new and long-term data for developing quantitative models and portfolio management methodologies

The vast majority of asset management firms now use models to predict returns on assets. In most cases, these models are straightforward and based on predefined correlations or other forecasting variables. Since parameter estimation in these financial models is data driven, they are inevitably subject to estimation error. What makes matters worse, however, is that different estimation errors accumulate across the different stages in the portfolio management process. As a result, the compounding of small errors from the different stages may result in large aggregate errors at the final stage. Estimation of parameters at the different stages must be reliable and robust to minimize the aggregate impact of errors.

The quantitative models produced constitute an integral part of the investment management process. Having robust asset allocation is one of the most important components, and decision making is frequently based on the recommendations of risk-return optimization routines. Fundamental to the process is careful definition of portfolio risk and return, making certain they are appropriate to observed or forecasted asset return distributions and underlying investor preferences. These concerns give rise to alternative theories of risk measures and asset allocation frameworks beyond classical mean-variance optimization. Equally important is the issue of how the optimization problem is formulated and solved in practice, especially for larger portfolios. It is also imperative to evaluate the sensitivity of portfolio optimization models as they relate to inaccuracies in input estimates.

Allocating assets is not only a major strategic decision, but it must be done in a cost-effective manner to obtain good, consistent performance. Given existing holdings, furthermore, portfolio managers need to decide how to rebalance their portfolios efficiently to incorporate new views of expected returns and risk as the economic environment and the asset mix change.

Optimal portfolio rebalancing requires consideration of two basic aspects. The first is the robust management of trading and transaction costs in the rebalancing process. The second is successfully combining both long-term and short-term views of future direction and changes in the markets. The two aspects are not distinct, and in practice they have to be considered together. By incorporating long-term views of asset behavior, portfolio managers may be able to reduce their overall transaction costs because their portfolios will not have to be rebalanced as often. Although it is complex to evaluate and model the interplay between the different aspects, disciplined portfolio rebalancing using an optimizer provides new opportunities to portfolio managers.

Quantitative approaches to portfolio management introduce a new source of risk. This is model risk that inescapably depends upon the raw material of historical data. Because financial models are typically predictive, they are used to forecast unknown or future values on the basis of current or known values using specified equations or sets of rules. Their predictive or forecasting power, however, is limited by the completeness and descriptiveness of the inputs and basic model assumptions. Incorrect assumptions and model identification, specification errors and/or inappropriate estimation procedures inevitably lead to model risk, as do models with insufficient out-of-sample testing. It is important to use models cautiously and to make sure that potential weaknesses and limitations are fully exposed. In order to identify the various sources of model risk, it is critical to review models against aggregated views of both new and long-term data.

c. The ability to monitor and manage risk across asset classes

In most capital markets firms managing risk is complicated by data distribution among a number of heterogeneous systems. The process of consolidating and normalizing data usually occurs overnight, assuming the processing batch window actually exists. The net result creates a significant time lag between the actual occurrence of risk and when decision makers can identify it and take action. Blind spots that prevent insight in traditional risk management systems can inhibit managing risk in real time. The shortcomings include:

- **Diverse infrastructure**: Most capital markets firms have multiple risk management systems for different departments, asset classes and geographies. The ability to share data is significantly compromised without extensive integration of legacy applications and multiple vendor environments

- **Volatility in market prices**: The velocity of today's markets is such that many systems are incapable of applying real-time market prices to positions and trades. As a direct side effect a firm's exposure moves with equal velocity
- **A lack of analytical flexibility**: Firms need to aggregate data across different dimensions to analyze data by asset class, currency, sector, geography, counterparty and trader. They also need roll-up and drill-down capabilities across these dimensions. Traditional data analysis tools cannot provide these capabilities in real time, as data rapidly changes and comes in multiple formats
- **Compromised alert capabilities**: A risk management system needs to continuously aggregate data and watch for trades or movements in the market that exceed established limits. Systems exclusively based on traditional relational database technologies struggle to generate real-time alerts since they are unable to perform the continuous computation that is required

Risk management systems must integrate with heterogeneous environments and support multiple aspects of risk, including the following:

- **Market risk**: Systems must aggregate positions, metrics and exposures across portfolios, asset classes, currencies or business units. They must also integrate live market data for real-time or periodic intraday mark-to-market positions. Finally, they must continuously compute a value range based on current and historic volatility, showing value by probability

- **Counterparty risk and limit management**: Systems must monitor limit utilization in real time. They must also apply business entity roll-up and drill-down capabilities with real-time mark-to-market analysis of positions and comparisons of positions to limits
- **Settlement risk**: Systems must monitor all open trades and track the current value of trades against transaction values. They must also factor in current market prices to value actual exposure. Finally, they must manage exposure against limits at different levels of aggregation, with roll-up and drill-down capabilities by counterparty, asset class, currency, trader, desk and virtually any other variable

d. The ability to provide back-testing of newly developed models

The increasing velocity of the markets, the tendency for liquidity to be spread across multiple execution venues and the lack of post-trade transparency present developers of trading strategies with unique challenges in ensuring the accuracy of back-test results. For example, potential FX trading strategies should be tested in a realistic environment representing actual trading conditions to avoid inflating returns or underestimating risk or liquidity. Additionally, simulation realism is more necessary than ever for back-testing all strategies, as traders increasingly use advanced execution algorithms to strategically enter and exit the market.

Because back-testing permits the development and analysis of trading strategies for performance and profitability, traders or quantitative researchers require the ability to evaluate the hypothetical profits or losses of a potential trading strategy using historical market data before they begin live trading with real money. Advances in computer performance and increased memory capacity now allow traders to test thousands of parameter combinations or strategy components against historical tick data and market depth. After analyzing the results, traders can modify their strategies and quickly test the modifications. Users can test multiple variations of a strategy simultaneously against the same historical market information, providing opportunities to quickly refine and deploy their models.

Back-testing is rapidly emerging as one of the most important aspects of developing a trading system. Created and interpreted properly, it can help traders find any technical or theoretical flaws and gain confidence in their strategies before applying them to real-world markets. A pivotal element of intelligent back-testing is not only the accurate simulation of the market conditions as a strategy creates an order, but also simulation of how the market reacts to that order.

One of the greatest difficulties in developing a tightly integrated execution/simulation environment is that it requires a seemingly paradoxical combination of being easily deployable out of the box, while allowing users the relative freedom to customize it, tune it and extend it for specific needs. Although back-testing strategies or market simulation environments can require widely different functionality depending upon the type of trading strategy developed (i.e., statistical arbitrage, automated market making, algorithmic execution strategy, technical analysis–based system), they all share a common set of core infrastructure needs that include:

- A multithreaded asynchronous playback engine that can precisely replicate the original timing between market events or accelerate and decelerate the data stream across multiple instruments simultaneously. Data playback should also be able to be paused/resumed and even reversed to step back in time for strategy debugging purposes
- Being configurable to receive inbound order messages, match orders according to user-defined matching logic and trading rules (trading sessions, order types, validation, prioritization logic) and deliver partial executions, fills, cancels, cancel/replaces or unfilled open orders
- Support for complex market data messaging structures such as full order books, object based messaging, client side caching and time series data
- Ability to aggregate multiple data sources into a centralized book or montage while maintaining the ability to treat each data source differently with respect to its quality, timeliness and distribution latency harmonics
- Scalability across grids/clusters to quickly test computationally intensive, high-frequency, high-volume trading strategies against massive high-frequency datasets

- Ability to combine playback/simulation across multiple assets simultaneously
- Granular control over the playback speed of historical data (i.e., playback at actual speed versus multiples of real-time speed)
- A means of collecting real-time data live, as well as the ability to integrate/import historical market data (either collected internally or obtained from a third party)
- Ability to process historical data of different quality and granularity levels, from fully transparent (complete history of market depth and trades) to very coarse (best bids and offers or trades only)
- Capacity to run trading simulations in either live mode with real-time market data or historical mode with previously stored data

Summary

Given these frontline requirements for achieving a highly tuned, real-time integrated infrastructure, the potential phases for migrating an existing production environment to the next-generation infrastructure could be defined as:

Phase 1: Create new platform with shared repository and live market data event processor

Phase 2: Implement real-time delivery into common platform

Phase 3: Migrate existing static and reference data into the shared repository

Phase 4: Establish post-trade analytics and reporting off the common platform

Phase 5: Perform real-time analytics against event processor and common platform

This stepwise transformation will ensure that existing production data assets are transformed and stored into a common optimized data repository and that subsequent back-testing of new models can benefit from multiple years of historical data.

Chapter 5

Drivers for Structural Change

ON SEPT. 9, 2008, the New York Times editorialized that the bailout of Fannie Mae and Freddie Mac demonstrated the need for better regulation of the American financial system. "As the housing bubble inflated, the Bush administration often claimed that America's unfettered markets were the envy of the world. But, in fact, they have sowed mistrust," the Times said.[1] Since then, of course, much effort has been spent globally to restore trust and confidence in the markets.

Future investment decisions may be shaped by new regulations that are more global than national and less tolerant of the old competitive dynamics of the financial services industry. One major change occurred before the end of 2008, as a number of investment banks redefined themselves as chartered banks. This in effect brought them under a different set of regulatory agencies than before.

Even prior to the worldwide financial and economic crisis,

the European Union was advocating a major shift to a principles-based, rather than a rules-based, regulatory system in order
to make Europe the most competitive economy in the world. In
addition, the EU has argued that principles-based regulation
should be the basis of a new global governance system, a call
that has been echoed elsewhere. The United Kingdom pointed
the way to such a system when it instituted principles-based
financial regulations in 2006. Then U.S. Secretary of the
Treasury Hank Paulson said in March 2008 that U.S. regulators
should consider adopting principles-based regulations and
accounting standards. Japan's Financial Services Agency issued
principles-based regulations in April 2008.

Principles-based regulations rely on principles- and out-
come-based measurements and prescribe only high-level procedures, whereas rules-based regulations stipulate a detailed
hierarchy of procedures, monitoring and reporting requirements. Table 5.1 shows the key features of both systems.

Hector Sants, the chief executive of the U.K.'s Financial
Services Authority, the watchdog organization presiding over
its principles-based system, has called the principles-based
approach "particularly appropriate given the need for flexibility
in a rapidly developing market, although we have not ruled out
the potential for more detailed requirements should this prove
necessary."[2]

Though it is expected to take years for the EU and the U.S.
to establish a common regulatory regime for capital markets,
the principles-based consensus has already led to collaboration.
As a first step, U.S. Securities and Exchange Commission and

Table 5.1: Principles-based vs. Rules-based Regulatory Systems

Principles-based System	Rules-based System
Regulatory standard is a simple set of principles – focus is on stated outcomes.	Regulations specify rules, procedure, protocols and procedures in great detail. Complexity arises from the attempt to cover all eventualities.
Firms formulate internal procedures to meet the standard and demonstrate capability to do so – flexible response is the goal.	Firms follow detailed rules and procedures that are assumed to have universal applicability. Demonstrated adherence is the standard
Principles and outcomes reviewed as per innovation and change in markets.	Results in relatively rigid process architectures and operations; not flexible in the face of change.
Recognition and incentives are correlated to demonstrated control and competence.	All firms are assumed to have know-how and competence to implement all procedures and rules.
Collaborative relationship with regulators.	Adversarial relationship with regulators.

EU Commission staff, assisted by the Committee of European Securities Regulators, will develop a framework for mutual recognition discussions. The mutual recognition process will also require consideration of a fair and orderly methodology for initiating discussions with the EU and interested member states, taking into account limitations on resources available for carrying out the relevant assessments. The working group jointly declared:

The U.S. and E.U., which comprise 70 percent of the world's capital markets, have a common interest in developing a cooperative approach to reducing regulatory friction and increasing investor access to investment diversification opportunities and enhancing investor protections. The concept of mutual recognition offers significant promise as a means of better protecting investors, fostering capital formation and maintaining fair, orderly, and efficient transatlantic securities markets. As we consider implementation of this concept, we encourage input from market participants.[3]

Implications of Policy-Based Drivers

As principles-based enforcement takes hold, senior management in capital markets firms will have to develop the capability to demonstrate accountability over the outcomes and build auditable workflows. This will mean improving cooperation across business, technology, operations, risk management and CFO functions. In its investigation into the subprime meltdown, the Senior Supervisors Group of the Bank for International Settlements indicated that coordinating risks and aligning required data and technology across the enterprise will be major challenges for some financial firms. "In firms that experienced greater difficulties," the SSG report said, "business line and senior managers did not discuss promptly among themselves and with senior executives the firm's risks in light of evolving conditions in the marketplace. This left business areas to make some decisions in isolation regarding business growth and hedging, and some of those decisions increased rather than mitigated the exposure to risk."[4] A heightened level of regulatory scrutiny and cooperation across international boundaries will create even greater urgency for better information management and decision support.

Regulatory and competitive pressures intertwine. In the U.S. the Reg NMS, phased in through 2007, has increased the speed of trading. The key is the data. Reg NMS requires a highly ritualized exchange of data in real time. Price quotes need to be time stamped and rushed to all other markets. Trading establishments are expected to automatically respond to arriving market orders within a second—turnarounds under 10 milliseconds, or ten-thousandths of a second, are fast becoming the norm—and quickly report trades and updated "top of the order book" bid/ask quotes. (Turnaround time is the time taken for a message to reach an exchange and return to the trader.) In this new world the winner in the hunt for liquidity is whoever can process the data fastest, according to market analysts.

How would a new regulatory environment in the U.S. and in Europe impact the new generation of risk analytics and risk management practices?

One banker noted that compliance might be a key issue. If proposed new regulatory processes are implemented, firms may have to show an auditable trail of transactions every 10 minutes, requiring an online repository of trades and risk measures. This will demand a large amount of storage, compute power and skilled manpower. There are differences of opinion, however. An IT architectural head at another large bank felt that the move to real-time risk and P&L was not a regulatory requirement. "The front office can't have a completely reconcilable real-time risk or P&L; for compliance, you just need to keep a picture at different points in time. Looking at the position is key," he said. Another banking IT executive said that the problem of real-time risk was about having a series of information models that meet standards to support front office data and streaming and P&L data, which is not sophisticated but is voluminous. The first issue is making data available for position management. In any case, given that there is a problem in measuring real-time risk and P&L positions, banks will need to look at the operations of their back offices as well as their front offices and create solutions that link front office risk and P&L.

JPMorganChase's Mike Ryan has underscored the importance of derivatives pricing. New derivative products are created with increasing frequency, and the ability to accurately price them is critical to future success. This has to be fast, literally millions of pricing calculations per hour.

Another IT executive noted to us that probably the biggest challenge facing banks is technical infrastructure. One bank is planning a 1,000-server grid for the middle layer of its expanding real-time system, he said. The application will pick up data from a bus, and the goal is to identify when there is movement in the markets and run calculations fast enough so that trading decisions can be made in real time.

The problem with such a system, this executive said, is that when it gets into 1,000 or more nodes, the administration of the workload breaks down and reliability becomes suspect. The 1,000-server grid was used to figure out if certain risk factors shifted that changed the overall exposure and whether market events that caused the shift could be isolated and identified. The experiment didn't work and within the limitations of time and resources more compromising alternatives were selected. The bank defaulted to checking all the data; risk was re-estimated on trades every 10 minutes, based upon the 20 or so trades done during that time. Even this took too long because there were thousands of variables to monitor. So the set of data that was polled and extracted was further reduced and some of its sort procedures were modified. Nevertheless, it still used a fairly crude method to estimate risk. This confirms New York Times reporter Saul Hansell's point, referred to in chapter 1, about feeding inadequate data into inadequate systems. The current goal within the bank is to move to a more scalable platform that uses only a subset of all trades. The work has only started recently and no new software application has been released.

To support low-latency algorithmic trading, formerly independent Merrill Lynch is considering a number of technologies based upon getting access to large amounts of market data and leveraging grids. Ajit Naidu, CTO for Merrill's Global Investment Banking and Institutional Technology division, said, "There is a need to have not only an extremely fast, reliable, scalable and redundant market access layer but also solutions for handling large volumes of market data. We are evaluating InfiniBand [a switched fabric interconnect standard for servers] along with grid computing to address the need for fast access to storage and the demand for computation cycles. We are evaluating not only large-scale database technologies but also how to query, filter and run algorithms on streaming data. We see a trend toward the need for global access to data and locality of reference and are evaluating WAN (wide area networking) data optimization using compression." Naidu also noted, "We plan to use grid computing for compute-intensive applications. These could range from algorithmic trading to real-time risk management systems. Grid is also being successfully used in the processing of models for market and credit risk."

As the financial crisis was gathering momentum, Ciaran Henry, Merrill Lynch's then risk CTO for Fixed Income, Currencies and Commodities, told the news service Dealing With Technology, "The challenge is that we are moving toward more sophisticated risk models. Our credit risk is now a full Monte Carlo simulation and it needs many thousands of data elements." This means "downstream systems need almost a super-set of all of the data of the upstream systems to perform these calculations." Merrill is "looking for a database that will support these requirements and scale for future needs." With its "evolving risk models it is also focusing on the need for improved enterprise data management within the bank."

At Merrill, Henry explained, "market and credit risk" are "where all of the cross mapping of counterparties, books, and instruments comes in." It accordingly behooves Merrill and other trading operations to look "quite closely at that space in terms of the next generation of databases and how we can use grid to put more space in there."

While traditional, nonelectronic trading volume has fallen by half, from 80 percent of trades in 2004 to 40 percent in 2008, risk managers as already noted are watching trading more closely than they did a couple of years ago because of the dramatic increase in both total trading volumes and electronic trading. Markets are also moving faster in terms of volatility in pricing and change in volumes. The Aite Group estimated in September 2008 that 7 percent of all foreign exchange trading is being conducted through algorithmic trading, driven by algorithms that represent both investment- and execution-based strategies. The volume of algorithmic forex trading is projected to double by 2010, according to Wall Street & Technology. Options trading has also grown dramatically. The result "has made calculating risk statistics an extremely difficult task for financial institutions, particularly for automated trading desks which need to scan the market for more than 1.5 million options records for volatility opportunities," according to Frank Piasecki, president and co-founder at ACTIV Financial.

The valuations of assets in the books are changing dynamically. This creates the need for "standardization of pricing and a capability to consolidate books for the front office across different systems," an IT architecture leader at a large bank said. As a consequence, risk managers need to see how traders are faring intraday and to know that traders are hedging appropriately.

The challenges can also be articulated from another perspective:

- How can you track the dynamics of the market in selected time periods and identify correlations between events and price behavior?
- How can you create a reproducible market environment

with an intraday market snapshot and time series data on quotes and prices that enables risk pricing in the same time window in which trades are priced?

- How quickly can you revalue assets and estimate balance sheet exposure when risk sensitivities shift due to market events?

The existing legacy data flows in most institutions today impede the visibility to real-time and historical data so that these questions can be addressed (see Figures 1a, b, c).

You need a picture of the market now and the market two hours ago, and if the portfolio value is down 5 percent in the two hours, you need to understand why the value dropped.

In the near term, firms are focused on consolidating risk for business units and delivering some level of aggregated risk in real time or near real time. The three main risk aggregation levels for business units are:

- Trade book level—intraday
- Aggregated level—end of day
- Portfolio level, with a risk calculation included in the valuation of instruments carried on the balance sheet

Meeting these challenges will involve rewriting many applications and changing the architecture of some key systems. In many instances, significant improvements to the front and middle office will be required before accurate P&L estimates can be computed. Current systems may not be able to capture all the

Figure 1a: Trading Process Flow

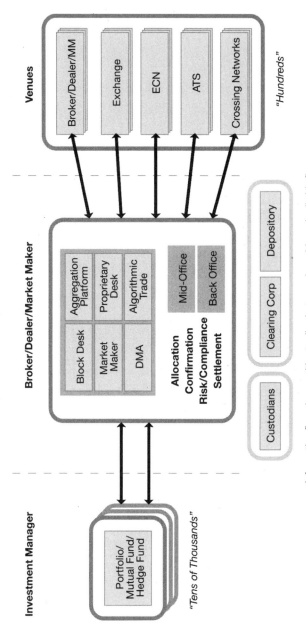

Information flows in securities trading between buy-side and sell-side firms, service organizations and trading venues that include exchanges, alternative trading systems (ATS), multilateral trading facilities (MTF) and dark pools.

Figure 1b: Information Flow in Front-Mid Office

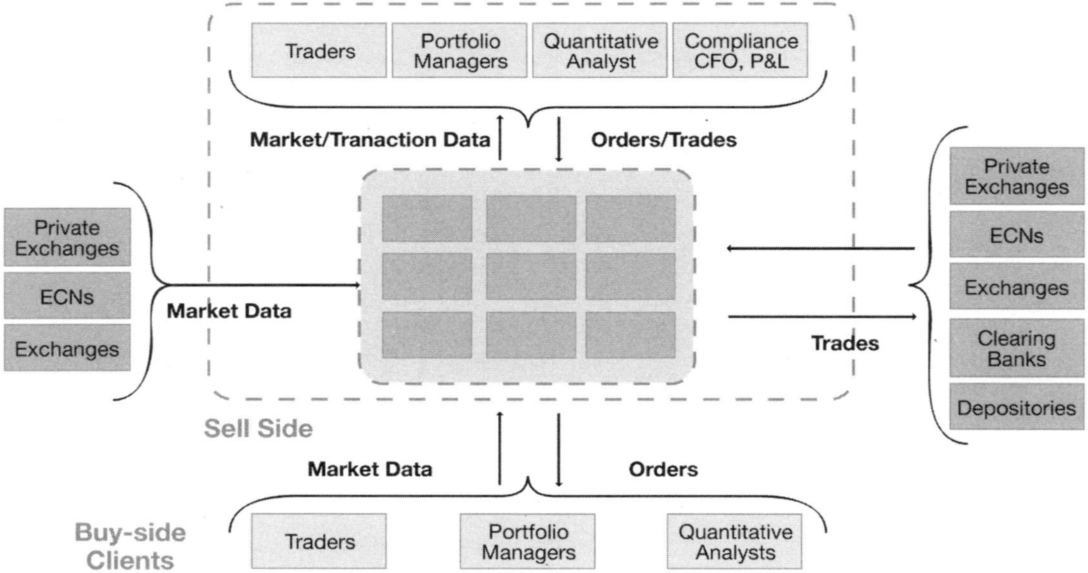

End users access databases designed to support specific processes that make up the trading cycle; to the extent that each process is supported by a data silo, the view of the markets and state of the portfolios will be different for each user community.

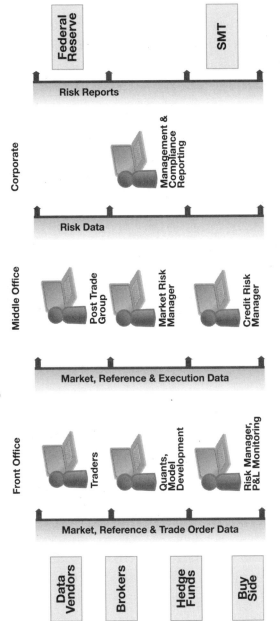

Figure 1c: Internal Data Flow Current State

Front Office

Traders

Quants, Model Development

Risk Manager, P&L Monitoring

Market, Reference & Trade Order Data

Data Vendors

Brokers

Hedge Funds

Buy Side

Middle Office

Post Trade Group

Market Risk Manager

Credit Risk Manager

Market, Reference & Execution Data

Corporate

Management & Compliance Reporting

Risk Data

Risk Reports

Federal Reserve

SMT

As data flows through the front office to the corporate reporting systems, visibility into the granular data is lost because of aggregation and reporting processes as the hierarchical structure of the heterogeneous data impedes access to the front office data in real time.

data needed for trades and P&L estimates, particularly when these estimates are most crucial, such as when there is a great deal of market volatility. In addition, handling front office risk demands intraday risk management solutions. Real-time solutions require new designs for application and data architecture, with latency and scalability as the key focus. Effective back office management may not always require real-time solutions, but near real-time, scalable solutions are a must.

Consequently, one set of design criteria for the next generation IT infrastructure will be the capacity to harvest related information from both internal and external systems and to streamline, aggregate and present the information to decision makers in a contextual framework. The emphasis will be on risk assessment and valuation at the portfolio and balance sheet level on a much more frequent basis than the current norm, which now may span weekly and even monthly cycles.

Low-Latency, High-Frequency Trading Drivers

Another source of pressure on the existing IT infrastructure, given the increasing volume and frequency of relevant data, is that updated information must be presented to applications very rapidly. From the early days of program trading to the current algorithmic applications, the development of securities trading technology has aimed at creating "first trader" advantages. As one senior executive put it, the goal is to "create and price differentiated products, calculate value at risk and perform other risk analyses" as quickly as possible. This executive estimated that a savings of "one millisecond of latency (time delay to make a trade) over the course of the year … could translate into $100 million in value" for his company. Information floods into automated, high-frequency trading systems throughout the 24-hour news cycle. Utilizing software programs that read, interpret and react to news items, a trade that is prompted in response to a U.S. Treasury announcement, for example, could be completed in milliseconds.

Responding to the growth in programmatic trading strategies by machines, in 2006 Reuters (now Thomson Reuters) began operating the Reuters NewsScope Archive, a computer-readable archive of its global news service. The service tags digital IDs to news events as they break in the markets, so that they can be downloaded for software to analyze them for relevance and deliver them for action. Traders linked into the comprehensive global news archive are thus equipped with information that is timed and stamped to the millisecond to help them identify events that affect their securities and better manage event risk. Traders looking to exploit market differences and generate profits benefit from drawing trends, discovering patterns and identifying correlations. The Reuters service has undoubtedly created new and interesting patterns in the incredibly complex field of event-triggered trading. Markets are constantly shifting and evolving and as soon as patterns are discovered they begin to decline in value as more participants make use of these patterns and early discovery advantages vanish.

A primary cause of concern about data inflow is the fact that quote message traffic in U.S. stocks has surged as a result of an increased number of derivatives products, sophisticated trading strategies, decimalization and Reg NMS. "We are all heading to microseconds," Andrew Brenner, head of the ISE Stock Exchange, a subsidiary of the International Securities Exchange, told a group of traders. "To be even a player in this game, you have to be in the single-digit milliseconds and you have to go down from there."

Escalating market data volumes are therefore having a tremendous impact on the worldwide market data community—from the producers to the vendors to the user community and the distributors. This trend will no doubt continue; just how steep it will rise in the future is a matter of concern for all involved. To stay abreast, or preferably ahead, of the growth in both volume and frequency, firms must upgrade their platforms for market data distribution into their internal applications without creating additional latency within their own environments.

Although exchanges have invested in excess capacity to keep up with message volumes, they are by no means immune to stress imposed on older infrastructure, and their reliability remains questionable. In September 2008 the London Stock Exchange suffered a serious daylong breakdown of its TradeElect system, which it implemented in June 2007 to boost traffic from 5 million orders a day then to about 60 million orders a day in 2008. TradeElect was the culmination of a four-year strategic investment. Its failure sent shockwaves around the capital markets as they wrestled with more types and sources of data, and struggled to determine and ensure the correct delivery speed of this data into and through an enterprise.

How Drivers Are Influencing Reference Architectures

Real-time enterprise risk architecture solutions are still in their early days. Many firms have been building point solutions for different applications and business units and have started to realize the challenges they will face as they move to a more aggregated view.

At this point, banks are taking different approaches to the design of the architectures they will need. Interviews suggest that not every bank will build a dedicated messaging bus and data architecture. One large bank has noted that the approach depends on the "trade types" that are included in the bank's main operations.

One innovation on the infrastructure side was creating the ability to build grid computing and data grid environments on demand. Investors within a bank need such a configurable application environment so that they can grow and optimize the size of the grid network as workload requirements change. If a real-time risk application had to be run at 2 p.m. or 4 p.m. and needed additional processing power, these environments could be built up and then reconfigured and repurposed later.

In terms of reliance on a messaging bus to move relevant data to the point of use quickly, the architectural approach is still suspect. Several apps in one large New York bank do near real-time risk management and a forecast, but this only works with a normal market. When the volatility and the frequency of events rise, such systems experience bottlenecks.

Banks are aiming to use a core risk management engine for market risk, credit risk, liquidity and counterparty risk. Many applications are anticipating and designing for end-of-day risk for Asia, Europe and the U.S. on a continuous, rollover basis off the same core system. Some global banks are reporting on counterparty risk by taking three snapshots a day; however, when done in isolation this has limited value in terms of balance sheet management.

The typical reference architecture in today's real-time risk and financial reporting systems is built in one of two ways. Data is either centralized into large risk data warehouses and pushed out to each system on a hub/spoke model, or presented by broadcasting all risk data out with specific risk systems capturing the data via a publish-and-subscribe subscription model. In both models, the idea is to capture the data and move it into a low-latency environment. Reconciled, quality data is provided to systems and users via one of these methods.

The historical problem with the hub/spoke model is that "TCP fanout" with software is too slow. With hardware, if a user subscribes to the fanout properly, it can set the latency. In the case of a multicast, or publish-and-subscribe (pub/sub), model, hardware can accelerate TCP, since TCP has an automatic pacing of the connection to an appliance and won't slow it down. The pub/sub model presents data out to users/systems via subscription. It keeps data moving, lets users/systems subscribe and can include larger systems/architecture expense. It includes a replicated infrastructure for each group that can include replicated feed handlers, data repositories, tick data and trade transaction systems. Pub/sub systems typically have a lower latency environment than hub/spoke systems, but this varies greatly according to system-specific design features.

Another approach is having compute power move to the data, which means increasing physical resources, such as processors and memory, where data is stored. This approach calls for combining the compute grid and data grid concepts and is yet to mature into a validated architecture and a range of products from vendors. Managing such an architecture will be more complex and the necessary tools far more sophisticated than what is available today.

In the quest for low latency many firms are complementing data services from Thomson Reuters and Bloomberg with systems that take data directly from exchanges to inside their firewalls. Latency issues extend across the trading operations cycle. "Not just data needs to be low latency, but everything along the order path needs to be low latency," says Larry Tabb, founder and CEO of The TABB Group. According to Tabb, the need for lower latency has led trading firms to rethink how they store data and where they set applications and to consider rewriting applications.

One approach to managing latency is to capture risk metrics and combine them with other market data. Volera/VoleraFeed, a high-performance derivatives analytics engine from Hanweck Associates, delivers low-latency, real-time implied volatilities and risk parameters for equity, equity-index and futures options. Delivered through the ACTIV Financial API, it covers the entire U.S. Options Price Reporting Authority (OPRA) universe of over 1.5 million option records, not including Europe and Asia. As a result of this strategic partnership, finan-

cial institutions can dramatically reduce their hardware foot-
print. The applications of automated market-making desks, sta-
tistical-arbitrage traders and risk managers can consume risk
characteristics as they would any other market data field and
improve on the frequency of the updates for these statistics.

Another solution is to create an aggregate order book.
Several vendors from the market data services and complex
event processing community have started marketing such solutions. The offerings are targeted at the companies' mutual customer base including leading banks, asset managers, hedge funds
and exchanges. These solutions are designed to operate on ultra
low-latency market data feeds and transform the feed data into
virtual aggregated order books to power smart order routing,
algorithmic trading and GUI-based trading applications.

In light of the two major drivers of structural changes, regulatory shifts and the explosion in market data volumes and rates,
it is possible to draw out the key attributes and characteristics of
the next-generation infrastructure for capital markets firms. The
key design attributes are:

- Continuous flow of data from active sources (internal
  and external to the firm) to the application environment
  where data is used for analysis and reporting
- Capability to operate on data as it is in transmission for
  purposes of filtering, validation and transformations
- Reduction in batch-based processing of data
- Capacity to instantiate application environments with
  required data sets for an application cycle

- Shared data repository with services around it
- Greater resilience of systems to ensure minimal impact on business continuity and recovery (see Figures 2a, 2b).

Investment firms that remain in functional silos using proprietary methods will find their supply lines restricted and will no longer be able to provide their troops with the right ammunition. Better-quality data, linked together to make decisions, is the new ammunition required to win the regulations data war.

Meeting the Challenge

The recent financial crisis has led to a re-examination of how financial markets operate on a global scale and how they are regulated. In essence, the current mood is to focus on the fundamental role the institutions play and the basic requirements in capital and liquidity to promote economic growth, rather than encourage expansion through leverage and introduction of more complex instruments. The core function of banks in the global economy is to facilitate capital accumulation and intermediation of capital to investment venues. Specifically, as noted earlier, banks:

- Acquire, service and retain customers to build a deposit base
- Allocate capital for investment to optimize returns and manage turnover of capital
- Manage the risks to capital

Figure 2a: Latency Along the Data Flow

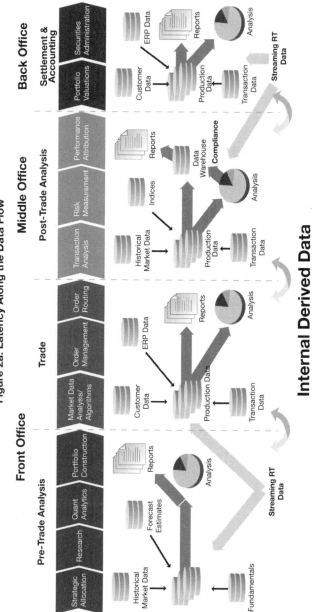

The consequence of the current architecture in silos is latency in data availability due to multistage, batch-driven movement of data.

Figure 2b: Market Data Management – Vision

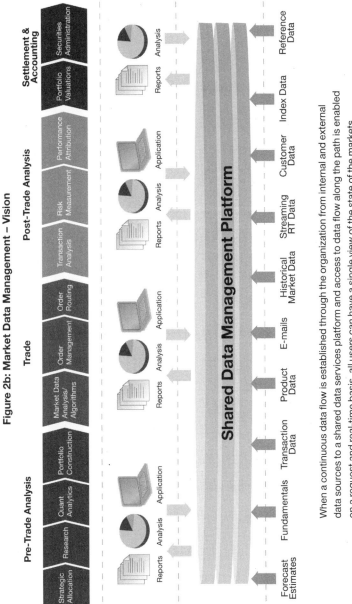

When a continuous data flow is established through the organization from internal and external data sources to a shared data services platform and access to data flow along the path is enabled on a request and real-time basis, all users can have a single view of the state of the markets.

Because these goals are coupled and cannot be pursued independently, management of the capital allocation process and the risk mitigation practices depends on a holistic view of the economy. When certain balances and relationships among factors that influence risk exposure, cost of capital and availability of capital are strained and cannot be assessed reliably, the likelihood of crises rises. The tight coupling between the last two items on the list above has once again been proven so critical that it may not be farfetched to claim that the primary function of a bank in the global economy is first and foremost to assess and manage risk to capital. This qualification is almost a prerequisite for successful execution of the other two. New regulations and supervisory regimes may underscore this observation.

Figure 3: Real-Time Consolidation of Data

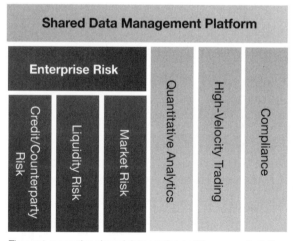

The next-generation shared data service enables a more holistic approach to building an enterprise risk architecture.

The new structure of financial markets that will emerge from the recovery and reforms will be shaped by a triad of new regulations, new methodologies and practices and new technology. Previous sections of this book focused on the interaction of practices and technologies, limitations and shortcomings that prevented successful risk management and assessment of risk distribution across asset classes and portfolios. Technology and improved design of systems and processes may help build a single image of data so that a holistic view of market activity, capital flows and liquidity and risk profiles can be made available to decision makers.

The successful financial firm will have developed a capability to understand, track and quantify risk factors across all portfolios and assets and a capacity for agility when volatility in financial markets rises. Mastering the data capture and flow and continuously transforming data into information, insight and profitable decisions will be the new competitive advantage, and information technology will be a critical contributor to success.

Notes

CHAPTER 1

1. "What We've Learned From the Market Mess." Bruce Wasserstein, Chairman and CEO of Lazard, Wall Street Journal, April 10, 2008, p. A15.

2. "The Subprime Solution: How Today's Global Financial Crisis Happened and What to Do About It." Robert Shiller, Princeton University Press, Aug. 4, 2008.

CHAPTER 2

1. "The Value of a Millisecond: Finding the Optimal Speed." Larry Tabb, Wall Street & Technology Vendor Perspectives Tech WebCast, June 19, 2008.

2. Ibid.

3. The TABB Group, LLC Westborough, MA, USA, 2008; www.tabbgroup.com.

4. "Innovation, Intangibles and Economic Growth: Towards a Comprehensive Accounting of the Knowledge Economy." Bart van Ark and Charles Hulten, Economics Program Working Paper Series, The Conference Board, 2007.

5. "Could Analytics Have Averted Credit Crisis?" J.R. Magee. RiskMetrics, 2007.

6. "Addressing the Data Aspects of Compliance with Industry Models." M. Delbaere and R. Ferreira, IBM Systems Journal, vol. 46, no. 2, 2007.

7. "Panel Discussion: The Compliance Conundrum." C. Chapman, M. Josefowica, E. Ealsh and B. Grossman, Insurance Standards Leadership Forum, 2004; http:/i.cmpnet.com/financetech/download/104-1532004ISLF_Matt_Josefowicz.pdf.

CHAPTER 3

1. "Sweeping Away a Sector's Chaos." Ross Tieman, Financial Times, May 28, 2008.

2. "IBM Solutions Offer Financial Institutions Flexible, Cost-Effective HPC Alternatives." Windows in Financial Services, Summer 2008, p. 27.

3. Larry Tabb, remarks during presentation on "The Value of a Millisecond: Finding the Optimal Speed," A Wall Street & Technology Vendor Perspectives Tech WebCast, June 19, 2008.

CHAPTER 5

1. "The Bailout's Big Lessons." New York Times, Sept. 9, 2008.

2. FS08/1: Platforms, March 2008.

3. Statement of the European Commission and the U.S. Securities and Exchange Commission on Mutual Recognition in Securities Markets, Washington, D.C., Feb. 1, 2008.

4. "Senior Supervisors Group, Observations on Risk Management Practices During the Recent Market Turbulence," March 6, 2008, p. 3.

Author Biographies

John Chen

John Chen has served as chairman, chief executive officer and president of Sybase, Inc., since 1998. Under his leadership, Sybase has become the recognized industry leader in enterprise mobility infrastructure. In addition, the company has significantly strengthened its position in data management and has a long track record of increasing revenue and profitability. In acknowledging his business leadership, Forbes magazine named John Chen one of the "Top 25 Notable Chinese-Americans in Business." He was named "2007 Ernst & Young Entrepreneur of the Year" in Northern California.

Chen is actively involved in international relations. He has testified before Congress on U.S.-China trade relations. In 2005, U.S. President George W. Bush appointed him to serve on the President's Export Council. In 2006, he was appointed co-chair of the Secure Borders and Open Doors Advisory Committee. In addition, Chen has been a longtime member of the Committee of 100. In recognition of his leadership in building U.S.-Asia business relationship, the California-Asia Business Council recently presented him the New Silk Road Award.

Chen serves on the boards of directors for the Walt Disney Company and Wells Fargo & Co.

Chen graduated from Brown University magna cum laude with a bachelor's degree in electrical engineering. He holds a master's degree from the California Institute of Technology (CalTech). He also has an honorary professorship from Shanghai University, honorary doctorates from the San Jose State University in California, and the City University of Hong Kong, as well as an honorary doctorate in business administration from the Hong Kong University of Science and Technology.

Chen is active in the community. He is a trustee of CalTech as well as a governor of the San Francisco Symphony.

Rich Karlgaard

Rich Karlgaard was named publisher of Forbes magazine on July 1, 1998. Before that he was the editor of Forbes ASAP, a bimonthly magazine covering the major trends and implications of the digital age.

Karlgaard joined Forbes in 1992 to start Forbes ASAP, along with the writer and futurist George Gilder and Forbes chief executive Steve Forbes. While editing ASAP, Karlgaard worked with authors such as Tom Wolfe, Mark Helprin, Camille Paglia, Peter Drucker, Robert Kaplan, Stanley Crouch, Esther Dyson,

Gore Vidal, William F. Buckley, Rosabeth Moss Kanter, William Gibson, Kurt Vonnegut and many others.

Before starting ASAP, Karlgaard co-founded and edited Upside magazine, a monthly magazine covering the computer industry and high-tech investment. Karlgaard also co-founded the 2,500 member Churchill Club, a nonprofit public affairs organization located in Silicon Valley. For this effort, he was named a Northern California winner of the 1997 Ernst & Young "Entrepreneur of the Year" award.

In 1997, as a hobby, Karlgaard co-founded garage.com with Guy Kawasaki and Craig Johnson; garage.com is the leading Web-based startup capital firm in the world, whose investors include Compaq chairman Ben Rosen. Karlgaard remains a board member of garage.com.

Karlgaard is a regular guest on CNN/FN's "Digital Jam." He is an acclaimed industry speaker and has written several Manager's Journal columns for the Wall Street Journal.

In 1998, he was named to Upside magazine's Elite 100 in the computer and communications industries.

Karlgaard is a graduate of Stanford University. Originally from Bismarck, North Dakota, he lives in Northern California with his wife and two children.

Dr. Raj Nathan

As senior vice president and chief marketing officer of Worldwide Marketing and Business Solutions Operations, Raj Nathan is responsible for all marketing initiatives for Sybase and its subsidiaries, Sybase iAnywhere and Sybase 365. In this role, Nathan leads a global marketing organization executing Sybase's go-to-market strategy and initiatives.

Prior to his current position, Nathan served as senior vice president of Sybase's Information Technology Solutions Group. Under his leadership, Sybase continues to be recognized for visionary technologies that meet the direct needs of customers and partners. Nathan was recently selected as a leader of the information technology industry by VARBusiness magazine in its "Technology Innovators: Top 50," for his decade-long commitment to Sybase technology innovation.

Nathan's work experience has taken him around the globe and has run the gamut from hardware to software, from large companies to small, including Unisys and Siemens Pyramid. Before entering private industry, Nathan spent many years in academia as a professor of engineering.

Nathan earned his doctoral and master's degrees from Iowa State University and a bachelor's degree from University of Madras in India.

Irfan Khan

Irfan Khan is a veteran of Sybase, Inc., with a tenure of sixteen years. As vice president and chief technology officer, he oversees all the technology offices in each of Sybase's business units. Together with the architects residing within the technology offices, he is chartered with ensuring that the voice of Sybase's customers and the needs of the market are reflected within the company's innovation and product development. In addition to his CTO responsibilities, Khan oversees technology evangelism efforts for Sybase. His evangelism group is responsible for seeding new products and driving new technologies within Sybase's most strategic accounts. Khan also is in charge of the Sybase Developer Network.

Khan holds a bachelor of science degree in computer science as well as a master of science degree in advanced computing from Kings College, University of London in the United Kingdom.

Sinan Baskan

Sinan Baskan is director of business development for financial markets at Sybase and is responsible for developing solutions for lines of business in the financial services sector. He has held various positions in the product engineering, professional services and marketing organizations at Sybase. Previously, Sinan worked at HSBC Corporate Investment Bank on risk analytics. He started his career at IBM Research Division. He holds a bachelor of science degree in engineering from Lehigh University, and master of science and master of business administration degrees from Columbia University.